WHERE IN THE WORLD?

WHERE IN THE WORLD ?

CHANGING FORMS OF THE CHURCH'S WITNESS

by
COLIN W. WILLIAMS
EXECUTIVE DIRECTOR OF THE CENTRAL DEPARTMENT OF EVANGELISM
THE NATIONAL COUNCIL OF THE CHURCHES OF CHRIST IN THE U.S.A.
CHAIRMAN OF THE DEPARTMENT ON STUDIES IN EVANGELISM
THE WORLD COUNCIL OF CHURCHES

This book is not an official document of the National Council of the Churches of Christ in the United States of America. It is prepared for use in study groups exploring changing forms of the Church's witness as a part of the long range study of the "Missionary Structure of the Congregation" authorized by the World Council of Churches at its Third Assembly at New Delhi; the North American section of this study being developed under the direction of the Central Department of Evangelism of the National Council of Churches.

Printed in U. S. A.
Second Printing
75 cents per copy
Distributed by the Office of Publication and Distribution
National Council of the Churches of Christ in the U. S. A.
475 Riverside Drive, New York 27, N. Y.

PREFACE

"Is the present form of church life a major hindrance to the work of evangelism?"

At New Delhi in December 1961, the Third Assembly of the World Council of Churches authorized the Department on Studies in Evangelism to undertake a long range study on "The Missionary Structure of the Congregation."

The title for the study had been suggested by D. T. Niles. As a key participant in the work of the Department from its inception, Niles was aware that over and over again study on the problems of evangelism ran into this major problem: "Is the present form of church life a major hindrance to the work of evangelism?"

The First Report on the Main Theme of the Evanston Assembly, "Jesus Christ—the Hope of the World," stated: "Without radical changes of structure and organization, our existing Churches will never become missionary Churches, which they must if the Gospel is to be heard in the world." Since then this conviction has grown. But if radical changes are to occur it is important that responsible examination of the required changes should be carried on on as wide a front as possible.

As a result of the action at New Delhi a widely based study process has been developed. Working groups, with representative biblical scholars, theologians, pastors and sociologists, have been formed in Western Europe, East Germany, South East Asia, North America. Smaller groups in South America, in lay training institutes and in pastor's conferences have joined the study. Requests for information and participation have run far beyond expectation.

To meet the demand for study material the Department on Studies in Evangelism is publishing "Concept"—a periodical for working papers and related articles. It appears now, however, that the time has come to give some order to the questions that have emerged in the first period of the study, and to bring the material together in a form suitable for local study groups.

It should not need emphasizing, that unless the study process being undertaken in these regional working groups spreads to local areas, so that the re-examination of the "structures" of our mission becomes the concern of the church as a whole, the study will be of little use. It should be said too, that unless the regional working groups can be fed from the thinking of many and diverse groups of those involved in the church's mission in local settings, it will be easy for them to lose touch with the realities of the present life of the church.

It is the hope of the W.C.C. Department on Studies in Evangelism (Dr. Hans Margull, World Council of Churches, 17 route de Malagnou, Geneva, Switzerland) and of the Central Department of Evangelism of the National Council of Churches (475 Riverside Drive, New York 27, New York) which has the responsibility for the study in the U.S.A., that the thinking of local groups will be constantly fed into the world-wide study process.

It would be appropriate to encourage small groups to form in each local church or better still across local church or denominational or racial lines to study "where in the world" the "changing forms of the Church's witness" should develop. Questions at the end of each chapter will help to focus the group's attention on the issues discussed in this book as they relate to the situations in your community and in your local churches.

One purpose of this study is to seek to prevent any deepening of the tendency to think that we must quietly bypass most local congregations in the movement to renewal. If there is much in present local structures that needs to be bypassed then let the Christians there understand why and invite them to join in God's movement for giving to the church a renewed understanding of her mission and more relevant forms for carrying it forward today.

Some important issues are dealt with in footnotes, and it could easily be suggested that they ought to be in the text. The reason, in most cases, is that the particular questions dealt with are more specialized in nature and it was felt that some readers could safely leave these questions to those more directly concerned, without themselves losing the thread of the general development. Finally we express the hope that in many cases the study process will become a "dialogue process"; with study stimulating responsible experiments in new forms of evangelism and with the experiments informing the continuing study process.

The bibliography at the end is a working list for study groups; not an exhaustive list of references. We mention too, several *films* which will serve as useful aids in the study. "The View from the Cross," has as its theme the search for new forms of church witness. It is of 25 minutes duration and is available from the Division of Evangelism, United Presbyterian Church, Room 1239, 475 Riverside Drive, New York 27, New York. C.B.S. in association with the National Council of Churches has produced a series of five half-hour programs in the "Look Up and Live" series on "The Mission of the Church." For information about these write to the Broadcasting and Film Commission, National Council of Churches, 475 Riverside Drive, New York 27, New York.

CONTENTS

STATING THE PROBLEM

1

STATING THE PROBLEM

"Without radical changes of structure and organization, our existing Churches will never become missionary Churches, which they must if the Gospel is to be heard in the world." (First Report on Evanston Assembly Main Theme)

"The average community is apt to be an introverted community which does not think primarily of its obligation to bring the knowledge of Christ to its whole neighborhood and to the whole world, and this introversion is apt to mark the life, thought and leadership of the whole Church. This applies to the younger Churches as well as the older." (Central Committee of W.C.C., Rolle, 1951)

"Only if our churches succeed in being with their laity in the struggles of our present world will the laity in their turn become genuine representatives of the Church in areas of modern life to which otherwise the Church has no access." (Report of Section VI, Evanston, 1954)

INTRODUCTION

The signs are out that we are reaching what can only be called "the crisis of the local congregations." At the seminary of a major denomination over 40% of first year students report that they do not desire to become ministers of a local congregation. It is reported further that there is a decline in students offering themselves for the ministry, and that many who could be expected to offer refuse to do so because they believe that to become the minister of a congregation does not place them at the point where the true frontier of the Christian mission is to be found. That frontier is in the world; but the local congregation is now so structured that it is a sacred island in the secular world, pulling individuals out of the world and causing them to act as commuters shuttling back and forth—leaving the world to enter Church, and leaving the Church to go back to the world, with no real relation between the two parts of their life.[1]

Many pastors of local congregations seem to agree that there is something drastically wrong with this basic unit of present church structure. They feel that the way the congregation is organized prevents them from fulfilling their primary roles as ministers of the gospel; that in the congregation their life is institutionalized in such a way that they are not free to be servants of the Church's true mission. They are busy—but not with the one thing needful.[2]

When attempts are made, however, to say what *is* wrong with the congregational structure, a foggy indefiniteness rolls in. There is general agreement that the problem is serious. This is indicated by the wide-spread response to the W.C.C. study—a response which by its world wide character makes it clear that this is not a problem just in one part of the world, but throughout the church. It is indicated, too, by the widespread interest (if not agreement) in books

---

1. See "The Relocation Problem" in "The Church and Its Changing Ministry," published by the United Presbyterian Church in the U.S.A. The whole book is important for this study. In a reply to a questionnaire sent to ministers in North America, one respondent put it this way: "The people of God, as they go into the world, park their 'pilgrim identity' at the door of the church . . . as they leave."

2. See *e.g.*, Joseph Sittler's article on "The Maceration of the Minister" from The Christian Century, June 10, 1959; and Samuel Blizzard's "The Minister's Dilemma" from The Christian Century, April 25, 1956; and both reprinted in "The Church and Its Changing Ministry," *op. cit.*

and articles on the subject.[3] When an attempt is made, however, even to state what the problem is, the fog approaches.

THE TITLE OF THE STUDY

The title, "The Missionary Structure of the Congregation," has caused deep misgivings. The key terms "missionary," "structure," "congregation," are each troubled by conflicting traditional and emotional associations, so that they do not immediately convey precise meanings. That indicates the need to clarify meanings as the study proceeds; but the title will serve its preliminary purpose of pointing to the right place for the study, if it is clear that two concerns are here indicated.

1) That we see that "mission" is the central concern for which the Church exists, and

2) That we must ask whether the present organization of the Church in local congregations is serving that mission or hindering it.

These two concerns are, in fact, the source of this study, and they found expression in "A Theological Reflection on the Work of Evangelism"[4] issued by the Department on

---

3. *E.g.*, Peter Berger, "The Noise of Solemn Assemblies"; Gibson Winter, "The Suburban Captivity of the Churches"; and the publication "Concept" issued by W.C.C. Department on Studies in Evangelism.

4. For the centrality of Mission, see pp. 14-15, "A Theological Reflection on the Work of Evangelism."

> "The commission given to the whole Church to be obeyed at all times and places is 'You shall be my witnesses.' Evangelism is of the nature and calling of the Church. It is a false differentiation to speak of the Church in its congregational expression on the one hand and its evangelistic mission on the other. The truth is not that the Church has a mission to the world but that it is God's mission to the World."

There has been disagreement about the way this is said—disagreement about saying that "the church *is* mission." This requires further study,

Studies in Evangelism. The first point provides the impetus for the study—it is because of our missionary calling that the concern arises. The second point provides the focus of the study—because there is a growing feeling that the local residence congregation is no longer an adequate form for the carrying out of this missionary calling.

THE PROBLEM OF THE LOCAL CONGREGATION

a) The Mobile Church

Most Christians today seem to hold an unexamined assumption—that the local congregation, centering around the homes of the members, with an ordained minister (or ministers) and a church building, is and has been and will be, the normal and basic form of Church life. Is it? Turn to the New Testament and you will not find it. There is no word for the "congregation." "The saints" gathered regularly; but there seems to have been a remarkable flexibility in the forms of gathering. They saw themselves as one body; one household; one temple; one building; but they gathered, apparently, wherever their secular life brought them together: in communities of occupation ("in Caesar's household"), in communities of residence ("the Church of God in Corinth," but meeting in houses), in communities of alienation (in the catacombs). For the first three centuries or more, they had no buildings, and in the early years there

---

but sufficient agreement for the present purpose is expressed, for example, in the statement of a Roman Catholic theologian's comment on the issue:

> "The missionary function of the Church is not one among several equally important functions . . . the mission is the highest of all functions in the sense that it is the supreme regulating principle of all Christian activities." (Quoted in Concept No. III, p. 37.)

For the problem of the present congregational structure, see "A Theological Reflection on the Work of Evangelism," Ch. IV, pp. 30-36.

is a remarkable flexibility about ministries and orders.[5] The important fact is that their gathering followed the realities of their secular life so that as their lives were swept along the currents of the world's affairs, their faith was given form at those points. They, as Christians, were on the move, taking the gospel to the ends of time and space, and declaring everywhere—in all the highways and byways—the purpose of God, already revealed and now being made manifest, to gather together all things in heaven and earth alike in Christ.

b) Changing Forms of Church Life

As the secular patterns of life altered, so did the patterns of church life. Finally, after centuries of having no visible "home" in the world, the adoption of the Church by the State gave an opportunity and a call for new patterns of relationship to and responsibility for the world. Now "churches" were built—but at first they were not "local" churches. Instead they were built at the crossroads of life; in market towns or at places of central government. From that pivotal point, Christians radiated out with a variety of "gathered" forms—often still in homes, but now too in social forms such as armies where previously there had been no opportunity to gather. But it is important to remember that alongside these new church structures that began to develop in the newly "friendly" world another form of Church life appears. If it is now possible to institutionalize the Church

---

5. See E. Schweitzer, "Church Order in the New Testament."

"The New Testament word for 'order' (tasso) came from military parlance. It was the term used for the swift deployment of a fighting unit from a marching to a battle formation. Order is the Church readying itself, moving out on its mission, in obedience to the Sovereign God. Different campaigns in the life of the Church may call for different tactics, and a quite different ordering. . . . On every level, and at every stage, order has a single purpose: to enable the Church to deploy its forces most effectively in its assigned mission in and for the world." (R. C. Johnson, *op. cit.;* pp. 20-21.)

in buildings to express the direct responsibility of the Church to Christianize the visible world of culture; it is also felt to be necessary to set up monasteries. These centers of Christian life—isolated from market and government and home and army—expressed the belief that the secular forms of life could not provide sufficient loci from which could come the Christian stream of life by which they were to be redeemed. The monasteries were erected to gather a Christian force in the wilderness to fight the demonic forces at the gathering points in the desert from which the demons launched their destructive raids on human society. The monasteries were erected to surround the exposed world of the city of man with the ceaseless life of prayer through which alone the constant tendency to decay would be stayed.

c) The Parish Church

The next stage came when at last in the Middle Ages the secular world settled down to that relatively static order of small local communities, where the whole life of the community could center around the local church with its local clergy. Here our familiar world of the parish and the local congregation with its central buildings and local ordained clergy at last appears. It, too, was a direct response to the changing patterns of secular life.[6]

---

6. Clearly it was a powerful opportunity. To have all of life centering in the Church—education, economic life, health, leisure—now made it possible to seek a visible expression of that ultimate purpose of God in which Christ's total lordship will be fully manifest. Dangers came with the opportunity, of course. In part, monastic life served as a reminder of these dangers. It is well, however, to remember one *great* danger. If the feudal period enabled the Church to create living local signs of God's ultimate transforming purpose for all life, it tended to obscure God's dynamic mission pushing out to the ends of time and space, crossing all barriers of race, nation, language and culture. This feudal danger seems to be connected with the failure in "missions," as "churches" accepted only local responsibility within their own region. Not until the nineteenth century was this weak-

This basic form of church life—the local congregation—has now lasted for approximately a thousand years. But over the last two to three hundred years changes, at first gradual but now increasingly rapid, have been occurring. Gradually the form of society in which life was centered in the local community has been altering until now in large measure *people no longer live where they live.* By an accelerating centrifugal motion, more and more aspects of life have been separated from the community of residence—most of government has gone, with advanced education, health institutions, business, communications media, leisure activities. To a great extent our decisions are made, our energies expended and our anxieties are formed, away from home.[7] The Church, however, is still centered on residence, and has this

---

ness (partially) overcome. It is important for us to remember this. (See Study III for a discussion of the question.) Now that we are beginning to seek to find forms of church life in different realms of modern society—education, health, etc.—it is vital to remember that God's purpose requires not only renewal within the different realms, but the crossing of barriers between realms, as Christ reveals his power to give all things their unity in Him.

7. Recent work on the development of leisure in modern society has emphasized the vast changes now appearing with the transition from a production-centered society in which men concentrated on producing enough to meet basic needs, to a consumption-centered society, in which there is a widening freedom of choices and increasing freedom not only in relation to time (with increasing leisure) but in relation to space (with increasing movement). The problems and opportunities opening up here are of great importance. To take one example: the movement of West Indians to London caused a political and social crisis leading to restrictive legislation by the British government. Most of these West Indians belonged to Christian congregations; but in terms of our usual parlance they "left" their churches when they migrated and found the problem of joining the church in their new environment extremely difficult. The congregations were of different colour and culture. What if the Church, in this increasingly mobile age, had developed forms which enabled it to use this crossing of colour and cultural boundaries as an opportunity to witness to the world that these transitions, instead of being the cause of a political and social crisis, can become in the Church a witness to the unifying and reconciling power of the grace of our Lord Jesus Christ?

time apparently failed to change its shape to meet the changing patterns of secular life.

d) The Modern Response to Social Change

That is not the whole picture. There has in fact been a marked response to the need for a Christian influence to be brought to bear upon those aspects of life now separated from the community of residence. That is why we have that remarkable phenomenon of Church Boards and Agencies: in particular, Boards of Social and Economic Relations seeking to influence governments and business; and Home Mission Boards to deal with a bewildering variety of tasks local churches have not been able to handle—such as migrant workers, prisons, hospitals and many others. We have seen also the burgeoning growth of "chaplains"—in armed services, education, institutions, leisure resorts, industry.

So too, there have appeared "Church and World" Institutes and "Evangelical Academies," seeking to train Christians for their life in the non-residential segments of modern existence such as vocations, government, science, education. The renewal of monastic forms of life, even in the Reformed tradition (Taize in France), and attempts to develop new "styles of life" appropriate to the changed conditions today (as in the Faith and Life Community in Austin, Texas) must also be understood in this connection. All these developments reflect the attempt to find shapes and styles of Christian living which will manifest the presence of Christ to men in those areas of life which are increasingly separated from the local community of residence and which for that reason are separated from the local congregations centered on the community of residence.

One strange phenomenon is that all those boards, chaplaincies, and "non-local church" forms are still usually described as "secondary" forms of church life. The real church is still looked upon as the local church.[8]

8. The strength of this "myth of the local" needs analysis. We often

Why is this? Is this simply a traditional response because we have been conditioned by a thousand years to think of local residence congregations as "the real church"? Or is there some better reason? Henri D'Espine[9] describes how in two Swiss Reformed Churches constitutional changes have eventually been ratified recognizing new forms of ministry, but there has been hesitation to ordain on the grounds that these are not ministries of the Church proper, but of Church institutions. So, for example, it is argued that a chaplain at a school or college cannot be spoken of as ministering to a true congregation, because he does not minister to the whole people of God—men and women and children of all ages—but only to a restricted age group and a small segment of society. But if that criterion is used, *where is there a true congregation?* Our local communities are now usually a highly restricted section—a particular class, color, language, cultural group; and related only to the residential aspect of the lives of that particular group. If the criterion should be that a congregation must represent the whole people of God, that it should reveal the manner in which the life of Christ tran-

---

hear "if it doesn't happen in the local church it doesn't happen." This, of course, is not true. Many of the Church's most important actions, decisions and programs take place at the level of "Boards" and "Agencies"—and this is necessary and inevitable in our complicated society. The strength of the local myth would seem to reflect the individualistic attitude which sees Christian life solely in the context of individuals at "home." This explains much of the equivocal attitude of Christians to their Church institutions. They have no way of fitting "Boards" and "Agencies" into their picture of the Christian faith, except as these are viewed as goads to push local Christians to be more truly Christian. They exist therefore, in this view, primarily because of the sin of Christians on the local scene!

This analysis, if at all correct, would suggest an urgent need for a reformation in Christian attitude towards the nature of Christian institutions and of their mission in relation to the other institutions of the world.

9. In the article "Ordination and the Diversified Ministries of the Churches," reprinted in "The Church and Its Changing Ministry," *op. cit.*, p. 118.

scends the barriers of age, of race, of nation, of class, of language; then the present local congregation singularly fails to meet the test.[10]

Has there ever been a time when residential communities have been so highly selective as in the present-day urban communities? As a result of the separation of congregations on the basis of residence has there ever been such a segregation of God's people into different communities of color, class, culture, and race? And since for so many of these people, many aspects of their life are not related to their place of residence, there is in the residence congregation this further restriction, that it is related to only a part of the lives of the members, as well as to only a small cross-section of society.[11]

---

10. Gibson Winter in "The New Creation as Metropolis," p. 134 ff., describes suburban life as a mass escape from the responsibility for a common humanity into little isolated worlds of limited conformity, so that the central character of suburbia is *amnesia*—forgetfulness of common humanity, of political responsibility and vocational conflict. When faced with the threat of common humanity (say in the threat of integrated housing) the reaction is often hysterical. The Church, whose true work should be *anamnesis* (memory)—the recollection of God's work in Christ through which God has created for us a common humanity—denies its very nature when it allies itself instead with this suburban *amnesia*. Implicitly, and sometimes even explicitly, this is what the Church is all too often doing by identifying herself in form with the isolation of suburban life. "The churches now have to ask about the structure of life within which the New Mankind can be embodied and proclaimed. The residential structure is no longer a structure amenable to this proclamation, for it has become the fortress against the New Mankind." (p. 140.)

11. P. Kraemer, in his article "The Urban Church: A Responsible Church?", printed in "Concept III," writes:

"His (the urban dweller's) everyday life is not concentrated upon one point, geographical or social, but revolves around a series of different points, spread over a broad range of relationships and territories. Without actually, or even supposedly, being a disintegrated personality . . . he leads several part lives, synthesised within himself. In the residential district only a partial, if not peripheral con-

It would seem possible that this explains why it is that the local congregation is "successful" in outer suburbs, but not in other segments of society. These outer suburbs are the places where people are still making a determined effort to make the house-centered home central, and who see the Church as their ally in their endeavour. Elsewhere, less attempt is made to center life in residence, and the residential church seems irrelevant to the main concerns of life. This may also help to explain why women, whose life centers more on the residence, are far more deeply attached to the Church. Even where the men are loyal, the sense of relevance is much weaker.

There is then a strong case for rejecting the conclusion that the residential congregation is necessarily the normal form of church life. It seems possible that the deep attachment to this view is holding the Church back from the freedom it needs to be re-formed in such a way that the presence of Christ can inform the secular patterns of everyday life. Hans Schmidt speaks of attachment to the view that the residence congregation is the norm, as "morphological fundamentalism." Hans Hoekendijik explained this as "a rigid and inflexible attitude toward the *morphe* (structure) of the congregation. Consciously or, more often, unconsciously, the existent forms of the life of the Christian community are taken to be fixed once and for all; their historical nature—

---

tact can be obtained with the totality of the metropolis; and a church which is making efforts to find an approach to the urban-dweller of our times should not be surprised if it is regarded and experienced by many as hardly more than a peripheral phenomenon. Nor should we make the mistake of thinking that this view is held only by non-believers. Many a faithful member of the congregation is often acutely conscious of the fact that his membership is in reality purely a spare-time occupation; it is an occupation to which he devotes—or does not devote—himself exclusively as a private person, according to whether he is willing (or able) to reserve a few rare off-hours for it, but which otherwise has very little to do with his daily social preoccupations."

and that means their changeability—are likely to be ignored."[12]

The case for saying that the Church is suffering from a local "edifice complex" seems very strong. Moreover, it would seem that the form of the local residence congregation is so turned inward, that it is often well-nigh impossible to reverse its direction in order that its life may flow outward into the structures of the world's need. Hans Margull traces this introversion to the historical origins of the parish system.

> "The parish system is based on the principle that Christians *come* for worship and instruction. The system arose simultaneously with the formation of a Christian society whose function was to form and maintain a stable "sacred order" within the given rural social structure. Quite naturally this system took no account of the situation which arose after the partitioning of the "sacred order" and the disintegration of the rural social structure. Therefore it did not know the need for Christians also to *go*. When faced with the *going* of the Christians, or of a new kind of gath-

---

12. Hans Margull, in an unpublished paper, has a discussion of "structural fundamentalism" which includes the following:

"By fundamentalism we usually mean an especially dogmatic position which makes no allowance whatsoever for a historical understanding of the Bible and Christian doctrine. . . . 'Structural fundamentalism' is a parallel phenomenon which consciously, or more often unconsciously, removes *morphe*, the form or structure of the congregation from the realm of historical consideration and questioning. In so doing it rejects the possibility of change and growth in structure. Perhaps it is wrong to speak of rejection as such, since the phenomenon of 'structural fundamentalism' is not as well articulated as its exegetical and dogmatic parallel; moreover, cases of explicit rejection are difficult to find. Rather it seems to involve a widespread but dormant fundamentalism in which structural problems involving Church and congregation are not held to be decisive questions for the Church. For this reason, this kind of fundamentalism is both more persistent and more understandable; it is present innocently in situations where the historicity of faith and of Christian existence is otherwise recognized and accepted."

ering for the purpose of going into the human sectors of the present industrial and pluralistic society, the very intimacy of the parish system emerges as the primary problem. It emerges as a "parish paralysis" which prevents the presence of Christians in a world where to be present means something quite different from the presence assured by the parish system in medieval Europe."

And Now?

What is now needed? Thought and experimentation seem to be proceeding in two directions:

a) First, there is the development of "small group" life (often called *koinonia groups*)—places where opportunity is given for the discovery of self-identity in the free and open meeting of persons. Here again, we may see two bases for small-group life: (i) around the Word and in seeking immediate awareness of God's will in prayer and mutual care; (ii) around a shared concern in the world—a neighbourhood, a common task, a particular problem. These are by no means exclusive bases. In fact, there is evidence that it is when these two centers coalesce—the "vertical" gathering around the Word and the "horizontal" gathering around a worldly concern—that there is a vital rediscovery of mission.

b) Second, there is a reaching out toward *a more inclusive strategy of mission*. There is a feeling that small group life is essential to a penetration of the broken fragments of our culture in order that the lost may be found at the scene of their lostness and there find meaning through the personal approach of Christ through the neighbour. Nevertheless the Christian mission requires more. It demands that persons be brought out of the isolation of the separated pieces of culture into the fuller unity of life in the Church.[13] There is

---

13. In discussing what is involved in the missionary command "to all nations," the W.C.C. document "The Missionary Task of the Church. Church Reflections," writes:

then the second major task. How can people be brought to a life of new unity across the separations of culture, class, race, language?

Several types of remedy are now being suggested. On one hand there are those who suggest that a unified plan to relate the structure of the Church to the various forms of our

---

"The term 'nation' is used in sufficiently broad ways in the Bible to warrant its application to peoples in their total linguistic, social, cultural and religious settings. The witness of the Gospel must be made to men as they actually are, within the groupings of nation, community, occupation, culture and religion in which they actually live. The whole structure of meanings found in such groupings is an inseparable part of the lives of those who live and work within them, and must be taken with full seriousness in the missionary task. It must be recognized, moreover, that these groupings and settings are always subject to change, and that witness to the Gospel must also take account of this.

"Neither sociological nor geographical boundaries are of ultimate theological significance for the mission of the People of God, since Christ has broken down the walls which separate men and groups from one another, and is fashioning one new humanity. It is, however, important for the Church accurately to identify those boundaries which empirically separate men from each other, since only so can the strategy of its missionary task be effectively directed.

"The Church is sent into the world, in order to gather men from every nation into the one household of God. While therefore it is an essential part of the strategy of mission for the Church to identify itself with men in their separate 'groupings,' in such a way that the Christian faith takes form within the particular cultural forms of their daily life, it is equally essential that the transcendent character of the Church as a supranational, supraracial and eschatological community be made clear. The Church of Christ, wherever and whenever it is found, has to exhibit the same marks of being the One People of God, with one constitutive history behind it, and engaged on one mission to the ends of earth and to the end of time. For that reason the mission of the Church requires both that measure of identification with men in their groupings which enables them to hear the Word of God in their own "tongue," to worship God within their own world of symbols and emotions, and to discover the way of obedience to Christ within the peculiarities of their own life, and also that measure of transcendence over the barriers that divide groups of men from each other, which will witness to the power of Christ to unite all things in one in Him."

pluralistic urban society is now necessary. So for example Gibson Winter suggests a "sector plan" which will allow the Church in an urban sector which is large enough to include a variety of classes, cultures, and sociological strata and small enough to allow for common planning, to develop a pluralistic approach to men in their residential, economic, educational, political and cultural life.[14] On the other hand, it is believed by some that such a unified plan is premature, that we have not yet even identified the places where forms of Christian life should grow, and are only beginning to learn how Christians can be the presence of Christ in the separated segments of our society. In this situation we must begin far more humbly. Coming out from the safe walls of our local churches we must identify ourselves with the concerns and needs of the broken parts of our culture, learning how to be the presence of Christ within that brokenness, and waiting for Christ to grant us such a share in his resurrection that we will see the Church begin to rise in new life, bringing forth also a new unity from the broken fragments of present day society. These people believe that we will need to be content for some time with a variety of small-group approaches.

Before we can discuss such questions intelligently, we must ask in a more thorough way, "What is the Mission?" and "What is the Church's place in the Mission?" After doing that we should be in a position to formulate these questions in a more satisfactory form.

---

14. So also P. Kraemer in his important article mentioned above "The Urban Church: A Responsible Church." So too the article by J. A. T. Robinson in "Bishops" on "A New Model of Episcopacy," suggests a "team episcopacy," with a group of bishops working together; one with oversight over residence groups, another over education, another over industry, but working together to integrate the approach to the various segments of life, in order that the unity of the Body of Christ may become manifest.

QUESTIONS

1. In our local church do we have a clear conception of purpose that permeates all we do? Are we sure that our purpose is the same as God's purpose for our Church?

2. Do you feel that something is drastically wrong with the basic unit of your present church structure? If so, or if not, explain your answer?

3. Where do we find our church falling short of expressing God's purpose or mission?

   a. Is it mainly in that our purpose is too small or too piecemeal at any one time, never all-inclusive enough?

   b. Do we have too few of our number *totally* committed to this *larger* purpose of God?

   c. Have we fallen heir to organizational patterns that tend to blur or obscure or take time away from the real purpose God has set for us?

   d. Have we gathered too limited a group representing too small a segment—not a cross section—of God's world about us to do an adequate job?

   e. Is our church too tied to its building to develop ministries at points of great need but far from this building?

   f. Is our church trying to do all of its work on Sunday
      —with too few hours of time committed to the work of the Church?
      —and working only when it can get a large percentage of its members together?
      —and with the thought that the ordained minister-leader can do most of the living, speaking and doing for the Church?
      —and forgetting that the Church is really the people of whom it is composed, who are to be the Church not only on Sunday for a few hours, but every day of the week, and every hour of each of those days?

4. In many churches women are said to be more active than men. In others, particularly the more conservative and fundamentalist, this is said not to be so. Why?

5. Are we seriously facing the growing problem of mobility of members of the Church?

6. What changing forms of our church's life are we developing to meet these changing circumstances?

WHAT
IS THE MISSION?

2

WHAT IS THE MISSION?

"It is the very nature of the Church that it has a mission to the whole world. That mission is our participation in the work of God which takes place between the coming of Jesus Christ to inaugurate God's Kingdom on earth and His coming again in glory to bring that Kingdom to its consummation. 'I have other sheep that are not of this fold; I must bring them also, and they will heed my voice.' This is His word to us; this is His work in which He is engaged and in which we are engaged with Him. For He whose coming we expect is also He who is already present. Our work until His coming again is but the result of our share in His work which He is doing all the time and everywhere. The Church's mission is thus the most important thing that is happening in history."[1]

---

1. From the Report of the Advisory Commission on the Main Theme for the Evanston Assembly "Christ the Hope of the World." This passage is from the paragraph on "The Mission of the Church." The whole document "Christ—the Hope of the World" is important for this study; and particularly Part II, "Christ and His People" and Part III "Christ and the World." Ecumenical studies often bear less fruit than they should by proceeding "de novo" instead of conserving the results of previous ecumenical studies. Those participating in this study should keep alongside of them such ecumenical documents as "A Theological Reflection on the Work of Evangelism" (Division of Studies Bulletin, Vol. V, Nos. 1 and 2); "The Missionary Task of the Church: Theological Reflections" (Division of Studies Bulletin, Vol. VII, No. 2); "The Lordship of Christ over the World and the Church"; and the Bulletins of the Department of the Laity. To order these and for further information on publications helpful in this study, write to World Council of Churches, 475 Riverside Drive, New York 27, New York.

In a questionnaire sent to a sizeable group of ministers in North America in connection with this study, correspondents were asked to react to the following statement by Hans Margull: "Being called out of the nations, the Church is called to witness to God's own mission to the nations and to partake in His mission. There is no such thing as the Church's own mission. Our mission can only be mission as being included in God's mission." A sizeable number objected on the ground that it is too humanistic to speak of God's mission. As more than one put it: "How can we speak of God as being sent? Who sends Him?" But this is precisely the gospel—that God sent His Son into the world, that the world through Him might be saved; that the Holy Spirit is sent to draw all men to Christ so that He might at last present us whole and entire in the family of God the Father. The heart of the doctrine of the Trinity is that it speaks of the fact that God has a mission. It tells us that it is God "who for us men and our salvation came down."

It is not difficult, however, to see the practical concern that lay behind the objections. There is worry lest in speaking of mission as God's mission, we may cut the nerve of missionary obedience. In an article by William Stringfellow[2] this is given direct expression. "Christians are fond of saying that evangelism is the work of God. I suggest that this is not so. Evangelism is the work of the Church."

Behind such a statement there is undoubtedly a justified determination to insist upon the Church accepting its full missionary responsibility: a determination to keep before the Church the ringing commands of Christ: "Go ye . . . and make disciples of all nations. . . ." (Matthew 28:19) "Ye shall be my witnesses in Jerusalem and in all Judea, and Samaria and to the end of the earth" (Acts 1:8). Nevertheless, we must not allow this essential emphasis upon the

2. International Journal of Religious Education. Special Issue on Evangelism and Christian Education, November 1963.

missionary responsibility of the Church and of all the whole community of God's people, to be taken out of its context within the mission of God. It is only as we see the Church's mission as set within God's mission that we see

a) its full shape . . . "As the Father hath sent me, even so I send you." *Our* mission is shaped by *His* mission. (John 15:12-27; 17:18; Romans 12:1-5.)

b) its true continuing source: "all authority in heaven and on earth has been given to me. Go therefore . . . And lo, *I am with you always to the close of the age*" (Matthew 28:18-20).

Unless the Church is constantly aware that it is not fulfilling its own mission, but is participating in God's mission, it will repeatedly forget that the mission is given its definition by God's missionary activity in Christ and that we are called to work in the framework of the *way* God works ("have this mind among yourselves which you have in Christ Jesus" Phil. 2:5) and of the *goal* towards which God is working ("He has made known to us . . . the mystery of his will according to his purpose which he set forth in Christ, as a plan for the fullness of time, to unite all things in him, things in heaven and things on earth" Eph. 1:9-10). It must not forget also that it can work within this shape and towards this goal, only as it allows itself to be the *instrument* of Christ fashioned for this work by the Holy Spirit (Acts 1:4, 8; 2:1-4).

These three aspects of our participation in the mission of God

a) conformation to the way God works—the *shape* of His mission

b) awareness of the goal towards which He is working—the *end* of His mission

c) participation in the divine life of Christ through the Spirit—the *power* of His mission, are aspects of one inseparable reality. This inseparable reality is seen, for example, in John 15:12-27.

a) THE SHAPE OF MISSION

The need for his disciples to allow their lives to be *shaped* according to the way of life revealed in Christ is given in verses 12-14, and runs as a firm undercurrent through the whole passage (v. 18, 20, 27). The shape of the life of disciples as they are sent into the world, must be the same shape of life as is revealed by Christ in his life in the world.

Development of this point is of great urgency for this study on "The Missionary Structure of the Congregation." The servant form of the life of Jesus, as he moved out into the world of human need, provides for us a well-spring of continuing *judgment* over the forms of our Christian life in which we daily tend to forget this missionary way of Christ and to fall back into the ways of the world. It provides for us all a well-spring of continuing release drawing us out of our hiding-places of religious self-preservation and worldly power, and sending us out again into the world of human needs.

THE SERVANT METHOD

The basic clue to the *method* Christ used during his life on earth is made clear to us in the temptations (e.g., Luke 4:1-13). The temptations centered around the question of the methods Christ was to use in his mission. In his baptism he had just received the confirming voice from heaven announcing him as the Messiah, and he had been driven into the desert to seek the answer to the question of how he would save the world. The temptations present to him *good aims*—they suggest to him that he can use his divine power to save the world by a direct attack on some of man's basic needs.

1) Luke 4:3 "*If you are the Son of God, tell this stone to become bread.*" i.e. Use your divine power to solve the problem of hunger, the *problem of economic justice.*

2) Luke 4:5 "*The devil showed him in a flash all the kingdoms of the world. 'All this dominion I will give to you,' he said, 'and the glory that goes with it.'*"

In the thought of that time, the institutions of the world—such as the state and the army—were under the responsibility of angelic (or demonic) forces. The temptation then, is for Jesus to approach his mission by taking direct control over the *political and military institutions* of the world.

3) Luke 4:9 "*The devil took him to Jerusalem and set him on the parapet of the Temple. 'If you are the Son of God,' he said, 'throw yourself down, for Scripture says 'He will give his angels orders to take care of you.'*"

Here the temptation is to use the medium of the most spectacular *mass communication*—of public propaganda—to convince men of his supernatural power and divine authority. Jesus' rejection of the suggested methods for saving the world by direct intervention in the realms of economic justice, political life and mass-communications, does *not* mean that Jesus was divorcing "religion" from these "worldly" concerns, and thereby telling the Church to keep out of economics, politics and public life! He who fed the 5,000, and opened his ministry by announcing "He has anointed me to preach good news to the poor, He has sent me to proclaim release to the captives and recovering of sight to the blind, to set at liberty those who are oppressed" (Luke 4:18), was clearly concerned with the problems of *economic justice.* He who said to Pilate that his power was given him from above and said that we must give to Caesar the things that belong to him; he who is called "King of Kings" and of whom Mary sang:

> "He has shown strength with his arm,
> he has scattered the proud in the imagination
> of their hearts,
> he has put down the mighty from their thrones
> and exalted those of low degree"
> (Luke 1:51-52)

is one who is fully aware of the importance of *political life* and of the need for it to come under the sway of God's purpose. He who called the crowds to him; he who rode into Jerusalem on Palm Sunday; he who commanded his disciples to make disciples of all nations, did not despise the need for *mass communications* to become the servant of God's truth.

The temptations were temptations because they did in fact point to some of the real needs to which God's mission is directed—*worldly needs.* It is God's mission to save the world—*"all things in heaven and earth alike."* The temptations are rejected, however, because they seek to meet these needs by the *wrong method.* The devil tempts Jesus to use his divine power to exercise his control over the world by open *self-assertion.* Jesus however rejects that method. He sees that he is baptized on behalf of all men as the suffering servant whose mission it is to save the world by *the way of self-effacing, humble, servant love.*

This becomes a central theme in the ministry of Jesus—to bring his disciples to the awareness that their participation in his mission must be through participation in this way of servant love. (Matthew 20:25-28; Mark 8:32; I Corinthians 1:18, 23; Phil. 2:3-11; I Peter 2:12-25.) So then *the shape of the mission* in which we are to engage is revealed for us in the missionary life of Christ. The importance of this for any analysis of the structures the Church needs for its mission in the world should be obvious but will need to be spelt out as we proceed. Clearly it implies that the church must allow itself to be drawn out to the places of worldly need; that the shapes of its life must answer to the shapes of the world's need. Just as Christ took on the garb of a particular time and went out as a servant to the particular points of human need, so the servant is not above his master and the Church must not be other than its Lord.

b) THE GOAL OF MISSION

In considering the "shape of mission" it is essential that we keep in mind the goal of God's missionary action. This is expressed in many different ways in Scripture. We use three:

i) The vision of the ultimate *reconciliation and unity of the whole of creation in Christ* (Eph. 1:9-10; 2:14; 4:1-5; 4:13, 16; Rev. 21:1-5).

The letter to the Ephesians gives us a striking picture of the goal of God's mission—the final unity of everything in creation within the one life of Christ. The life of Christ is seen as a powerful force of unity breaking through all the hostile divisions within the human family and within the world of creation. This is now seen to be the secret purpose of creation—a secret which God has at last unveiled in Christ—as we can look forward with certainty to the ultimate unity of all things within Christ's love (3:7-21).

In chapters 4, 5 and 6, the implications of this for the present life of the Christian community are drawn out. The "unity of the Spirit" is manifested in the community life of the Church (4:1-16). We would be wrong to think of this new life as being lived in a churchly institution isolated from the life of the world. In 4:17 following it is made clear that this life in the unity of the Spirit is lived out in everyday human situations within the institutional life of the world. This in fact is what Christian life is meant to be—a break through of Christ's way of unity into the old world of division and hostility. Because the Christian life is a casting away of the sins which cause division (4:22-32) it results in infusing the structures of the world with the unity of life in Christ (in the family 5:22ff and in master-slave relations 6:5ff).

A summary of the meaning of this unity of life in Christ in the face of the divisions and hostilities which mark the life of the world is given in Col. 3:11-15: "Here there cannot be Greek and Jew (the dividing wall of nation and race), circumcised and uncircumcised (the barriers of religiousness), barbarian or Scythian (the clash of cultures), slave, free man (the hostilities of class), but Christ is all in all." The "missionary structure" of the life of the Church should be such as to allow the unifying power of Christ to be manifest at the points where the hostilities of nation, race, culture, religiousness, class, are destroying the unity of God's creation. The missionary structures must serve Christ in such a way that his healing resources shall be released at the points of the world's sorest needs.

THE REFLECTION OF THE GOAL IN THE PRESENT

What does this say concerning our present structures? Would it not appear that our present congregations based on residence are desperately inadequate to be the avenue of this mission of Christ? Are not modern urbanized residence communities the most subtle devices ever created to separate men from each other along these lines of separation—race, class, culture, nation, religion? Does not a church pattern which structures Christians within residence communities tend to deepen those worldly separations rather than bring the uniting reconciling power of Christ to bear in such a way that these worldly barriers collapse and Christ's ultimate purpose is revealed? Is it not true that in our world in varying degrees men do come together across these barriers in other activities of life—at work, in politics, in health, in mass entertainment—but that church life is related to men at the place of their greatest separation (residence), and takes on very little form at the places where the world gives an opportunity to break through these separations? It would seem then that the Church in modern urban life is denying itself the structures necessary to express the unifying power of life in Christ.[3]

ii) *The vision of the realization of the full potentialities of all creation.* Karl Barth uses two phrases which give clear expression to the inseparable relation of God's work of redemption to his work of creation. "Creation is the external basis of the covenant." "The covenant is the internal basis of creation." The vision of creation given in Genesis is of man, the obedient son of God, exercising dominion over

---

3. A Biblical symbol that lies in close relation to the symbol of unity, is that of peace (Shalom). Ephesians speaks of "the unity of the Spirit in the bond of peace," and the word "peace" provides us with another way of tracing out *the missionary goal* which God has revealed to us in the coming of Christ and in the sending of the Holy Spirit. This is spelled out in "A Theological Reflection on the Work of Evangelism," p. 6:

"The Gospel is the story of God's redeeming work in Jesus Christ. The spread of the Gospel is God's chosen way to establish His triumphant rule over mankind. Gospel and man are meant for each other. They belong together. The Gospel of God's Kingdom is a Gospel for the nations.

"This King has willed to rule as Savior. Wherever His Kingship is proclaimed, His saving concern for mankind will be made manifest. The end of this saving concern is the gift of peace, the establishment of 'shalom.' To receive God's shalom is to enter into an inheritance where many things belong together—mercy and truth, righteousness and peace, goodness and plenty, man's salvation and God's glory. In shalom, peace is established between God and man in atonement and reconciliation, so that man is saved from the terrifying presence of an unknown mystery and is made a partner in God's covenant; peace is established between man and his neighbor, so that society is saved from destructive selfishness and men are established in community; peace is established between a man and himself, so that he is saved from dividedness and is restored in his integrity as made in the image of God.

"This shalom is in Jesus Christ in whom God has proclaimed His Gospel. By this proclamation is created a new situation for mankind because, whether acknowledged or unacknowledged, it brings mankind into a decisive relationship with God."

creation by using his creative capacities to bring out nature's full potential and by using this fruitful world of nature as the arena for the development of the full social and personal capacities of the human family (Gen. 1:26-28; 2:15). Because man has turned away from God he has fallen out of true relationship to himself (3:7); out of harmony with God (3:8-9); out of unity with his human partner (3:12); and also into disharmony with the world of nature (3:16-17). But it is precisely these distortions *in the world* with which redemption is concerned.[4]

In Colossians Paul draws a parallel between Christ's work as creator and redeemer (Col. 1:15-17 and 18-23). It is the same world to which Christ is related in both cases. When Christ comes as "the Second Adam," it is to overcome *all* the divisions expressed in Genesis 3. That is why his *miracles* are concerned not only with man in his inwardness ("Son thy sins are forgiven"); but just as much in his body, in his community, and in his relation to nature. Christ is the Savior of *the world.* He walks on the water as the sign of

---

4. "A Theological Reflection on the Work of Evangelism" expresses this point:

"When it describes the mighty deeds of God, the New Testament uses political, juridical, sociological and other secular terms. Kingdom of God, Son of David, King of the Jews; Redemption, Faith, Forgiveness; Healing, Freedom, Service—all such words by which the person and work of Jesus Christ are described are secular words. This secular terminology of the New Testament is not only a form of speech. For the coming of Jesus Christ in the flesh and in the power of the Spirit is a 'secular' event. It is an event in the world and for the world.

"For many, however, the language and message of the Bible have become merely 'religious.' It is the task of evangelism to discover and to proclaim the Gospel in its specific, concrete, unique and secular sense. The ministry of the evangelist is to announce that all events happen within and take meaning from the Gospel facts. He pronounces that the promised Messiah-King has come, that He is given full power over heaven and earth, and that the Holy Spirit is being poured out over all flesh as an earnest of the final consummation."

his Lordship over nature; he feeds the 5,000 by his
of nature and heals men's bodies as a sign of his
heal the wounds of his created world. Whereve
hurt, there is the Savior.

THE SERVANT FORM OF THE CHURCH

What does this mean for the missionary structure of the Church? How can her life be so ordered that it may bring to visibility the healing power of Christ at those points where the divisive results of our separation from God are most apparent?

It would seem here that if the Church is to be the servant of God's mission, it must (like Christ) be sensitive to the points of disjunction in the world, and be so structured that it focuses the obedience of the Christian community at these points of need, bringing the healing resources of Christ to bear in such a way that his forgiveness and love are thrown across the chasms of separation. It would seem too, that this obliges Christians to use to the full the "secular" means God offers us in the world to discern "the structures of need" and to match them with the structures of Christian community.[5] What, for example, does this mean for the church's "necessary structure" in relation to the problem of race conflict, the nuclear problem, the "youth culture"?

iii) *The awareness that the final goal has already been*

5. "A Theological Reflection on the Work of Evangelism," p. 6:
"Christian obedience is the result of Christian conversion. But, once the will is surrendered to Christ's obedience, theological reflection can shed light on all that obedience involves. To such theological reflection, in its work of evangelism, the Church is summoned anew today to understand what God is doing in these times through all the changes that are taking place in the ways and circumstances of human life, to penetrate into the significance of the new forms of association in which persons find their social satisfaction, to ask how the Gospel may be related to men in their several needs as they seek to come to terms with life."

revealed in Christ, but will not be fully manifest until Christ returns to complete his new creation. i) and ii) must be kept within this framework provided by iii) or they run the danger of suggesting that we can look forward to a gradual unfolding of God's plan—a progressive rolling back of the shadow side until we emerge into the full light of the sun. Not so. Our place in God's mission in this "time between the times"—the time from Christ's incarnation until his parousia (his return)—is to be witnesses to Christ. By word and deed members of the Christian community are called to be "signs" of Christ's purpose, so that the world can see in our word and deed what God's purpose is, and so will be ready when he comes at last to "give us the Kingdom," and create the "new heaven and a new earth." The final goal suggested in i) and ii) has already been revealed by Christ. Now in this time of delay before he establishes this Kingdom in open victory, time is given for men to hear the truth (how can they hear unless we preach), and to learn to practice Christ's way (how can they do that unless they see Christ the light as reflected light in the community life of disciples in the world). Life in the Spirit is an "earnest," a "downpayment," on the final gift of the perfect life of Christ which he shall give us when he returns. In the meantime the task of the Church is to be used by Christ to set up "signs" in the world by word and deed—signs which make visible Christ's ultimate purpose at the places where the world seems most separated from the life of God.

> "There can be no distinctive witness where there is no distinctive life. Christians are, therefore, called to repentance. They must come to Christ the Servant and let Him put His distinctive form upon them. They must care that the Church which evangelizes must also give visible evidence of the credentials for its work. But besides these credentials, men will also ask for signs. Signs there will be.

> Sick people will be healed, prisoners will be visited, lonely men will find fellowship, estranged people will be reconciled, worthless people will get a new value. However, neither herald nor hearer must forget that these signs only point to God and His presence with His Church. As it is written: 'And they went forth and preached everywhere, while the Lord worked with them and confirmed the message by the signs that attended it.' Therefore must the evangelist always seek to press for a faith beyond all signs in the faithful Giver Himself. His command and His promise are, 'Seek His Kingdom and these things shall be yours as well.'"[6]

This eschatological perspective has important implications for our understanding of the Church's life in the present. The fact that our present life is not a final expression of victory, and that here we have "no abiding city," but that we seek one still to come, means that no structure of church life either in the realm of church *order* or of church *thought* (theology) can claim eternal validity. Just as Christ took form within the changing structures of history, and put on a particular garb, spoke a particular language, and related himself to a particular government and particular social problems, so he requires of his people that they take on similar particularity.

It is important for us to remember that this is not only true of church order—congregational forms; ways of ministry—but is also true of church thought. A Christian theology, to be Christian, must be a reflection on what God is doing.[7] The "past" character of Christian theology because of the fact that it is rooted in God's deeds and words, often misleads us into assuming that we can formulate theology in such a way that it will be just as "true" 100 years

---

6. "A Theological Reflection on the Work of Evangelism," pp. 18-19.

7. See "A Theological Reflection on the Work of Evangelism," p. 6, as quoted above.

from now as it will be today. To think this way is to forget that the "past" revelation speaks to us of a living God who is continuously at work in history and calls us to respond to his work in the world. It is for this reason that we must resist the common tendency to separate theology from worldly disciplines such as sociology and psychology. Just as we must reject the tendency to treat Church and world as though they were separate entities, so we must reject the separation of the theological task from the sociological. It is within this world that the theological task must be carried on.[8]

---

8. What this means for theological education is an urgent question. There has been too great a tendency to separate the "theological" and "practical" disciplines; and to separate the seminary world from direct responsibility for the Church's mission in the world. However, the oft-heard sneers from parish ministers concerning the ivory-tower character of seminary education is a false expression of the problem. Both *parish* and *seminary* share in the false separation of the Church from the world; and both are called to repentance.

The problem for the seminary is made more acute by the dissatisfaction of so many students with the present "parish ministry." For the most part the seminary curriculum assumes that the structures in which theological students will work can be taken for granted. The seminary's task is assumed to be mainly that of giving the students mastery over

i) the "given" content of the Christian faith

ii) the practical techniques for a traditional type ministry—Christian education for the local parish; preaching in monologue form from the pulpit; church administration in the parish setting. Even the new practical disciplines like counselling do not question the adequacy of the witnessing forms of the church's life.

This view of seminary training is viable only when the forms of witness in the church are considered to be viable and therefore not requiring reflection. But when there is apparent need for major reformation of the witnessing relation of the church to the world, what then is the task of the seminary? If it is meant to give theological guidance to the church as she seeks to fulfill her mission, then her present curriculum and relation to church and world would appear to be inadequate.

It would seem to be required of seminaries that they accept the theological responsibility of carrying on the present training of ministers in dialogue with the present re-assessment of the witnessing forms of the church's relation to the world. What form this dialogue will need to take is a major question. It may mean that seminaries will need to be

c) THE POWER OF THE MISSION

Having spoken of the shape of mission—its servant character; the goal of mission—the final unity of all in the peace of Christ; we must turn finally to the power of mission as expressed in the gift of the Holy Spirit at Pentecost.

---

involved in experimental forms of mission. It may mean an interweaving of "content" and "practice" in the curriculum to an extent not previously attempted. It may mean a new relation to "lay" training centers. One can only plead that seminaries accept some real responsibility in this rethinking. If the church has "mission" as the central "mark" of her life, the seminary must allow that mission to control her training of the ministry; and if that missionary relationship must now be radically re-assessed, the seminaries must see that her structures are no less in question than those of the local residence congregation. Moreover, her responsibility for leading in the re-appraisal is integral to her calling.

In an unpublished article on "The Problem of Education for the Ministry," Gibson Winter, after stating his belief that "seminaries can only be viable structures of training if they participate in the missionary task for which they are educating their students," goes on to suggest some of the necessary elements for "a dialogic framework of preparation." He suggests e.g.,

i) "Theological reflection and ministering can no longer be insulated from one another—the one in the seminary precincts and the other in the parochial institutions of another age."

ii) There needs to be faculty involvement, "at crucial points with the men whom they are preparing for the ministry and focused around the specific role of their own discipline in the mission of the Church."

iii) "The development of the Church's ministry cannot be confined any longer to a training of clergy in isolation from laity. . . . There can and should be, of course, periods of theological work in the quiet of an academic situation, but such reflection becomes integral to training for the ministry when it is set in the larger context of such objective involvement in mission and ministry."

iv) "Training for the ministry is training in apostolate and servanthood. It can no longer be conducted in isolation from that context; in fact, ministry and mission are actually to be developed in the process of training, and this is the joint task of faculty, students, pastors and laymen."

Gibson Winter suggests that just as clinical training has developed in the area of pastoral care, so we need similar dialogue settings in the framework of the church's mission—*e.g.,* urban training centers.

We would suggest that Winter has raised the right questions. Now we must press upon seminaries the need to search for workable answers.

Henderik Kraemer is fond of saying that the very moment of the Church's birth at Pentecost, was also the moment that the missionary task was born. The descent of the Spirit made the disciples apostles, i.e., missionaries. Pentecost is the fulfilment of the promise: "You shall receive the power of the Holy Spirit and you shall be my witnesses." (Acts 1:8)[9]

In the Pentecost story we are given in historical event form all that we have been drawing out above in doctrinal form from gospels and epistles concerning the shape and goal of mission.

Just as in the miracle of the Incarnation God granted us a vision of the perfect human life which he has planned for us and towards which he is drawing us, so, at Pentecost, in a second miracle, he granted us a perfect expression in miniature of the new society he has planned for us and toward which he is leading us.

If in Ephesians we are given a glowing mental vision of the unity of all in creation in Christ; if in Colossians we are caught up in the poetic vision of life in Christ breaking through the barriers of nation, race, culture, religion, class and uniting all within the perfect love of Christ; on the day of Pentecost we see the power of the Spirit breaking into history to make this vision a reality. The barriers of language, race, and culture fell before the rush of the Spirit breaking into the life of the world there in the streets of Jerusalem (Acts 2:43-47). The new life that was created broke through the barriers of class and possession, creating a community of divine unity from above. (*Koinonia* [fellow-

9. Notice, too, that in John's Gospel the prayer of Christ in Chapter 17 asking that his disciples be sent to the world in the same way that he had been sent, becomes an actuality in John 20:21-22 with the gift of the Holy Spirit. "As the Father hath sent me, even so send I you. And he breathed on them, and said to them 'Receive the Holy Spirit.'" In Matthew's Gospel the Great Commission (28:18-20) similarly puts the missionary obedience of the Church within the enabling framework of God's action: "And lo I am with you always."

ship] means those who share in a gift: here the gift of the Holy Spirit. The life of the shared gift at Pentecost revealed that the power of the Spirit is able to break down the barriers that prevent true human sharing; so creating there the perfect fellowship of the shared love of God towards which God is leading us.)

The perfection of Pentecost stands as a vision of the goal towards which the Spirit guides us, and as a reminder of the conditions we must meet if we are to enter into the life of the fellowship of the Spirit. The disciples received the Spirit in all his fulness because they were all together, of one mind, in one place, waiting, expectant, surrendered, ready to do God's will. Those conditions have never been perfectly fulfilled, but because they have been often repeated in part, the succeeding years have seen many partial expressions of the final outcome of history of which Pentecost is the perfect miniature sign.

In the next study we will look again at the Pentecost story to see what it tells us of the permanent "marks" of Church life—the need to wait on God in attendance on Word and Sacrament, in prayer and Bible study. Here we simply notice that this story makes it clear that any Church structures which serve the mission of the Church must be such that they enable Christians together to be open to the Spirit's power to unite them across the barriers in society. This emphasis, however, must be combined with all we have seen above concerning the Shape of the Mission and the Goal of the Mission. The Holy Spirit's task, as John's Gospel makes clear, is to take the lives of disciples and train them in the life of Christ—constantly elucidating for them the truth of Christ in changing circumstances, and teaching them to "observe" (i.e. to work out in their lives) the whole teaching of Christ. The Holy Spirit enables us to grow up into the fulness of the life of the Body of Christ, and so to be fully the servants of Christ in the world, seeking to be the avenues of his healing, unifying and fulfilling love at the points of the world's greatest need. The "missionary structures" of the Church must be the structures best suited to the service of this mission of God.

QUESTIONS

1. What do we mean by "mission"?
2. How does the New Testament describe the mission of God in the world? What is the relation of the Church to this mission?
3. Study Paul's favorite picture of the Church as the "body of Christ," the continuing incarnation. (See Acts 9:15; I Corinthians 10:17; 12:12-27; Romans 12:1-5; Ephesians 1:22, 23; 4:13; John 17:18; 14:12; Colossians 1:18; 2:17-19; 4:15-17; Galatians 2:20.) What does this have to say about the mission of God and the place of the Church in God's mission?
4. What methods did Christ refuse to use to reach his goal or achieve his purpose? (See accounts of his temptation in Matthew 4:1-11 and Luke 4:1-13.) Does this say anything about unworthy means of evangelism?
5. What methods did Christ use to achieve his goal? Are these the most effective methods for his Church to use?

6. If ministry and mission are accepted as God's purpose for his Church and each of its members, should the emphasis in many of our church activities change (organizational meetings, class and teaching, worship and preaching?) or be redirected that members might be trained to be witnesses in their family, business and industrial relations, politics and international affairs, race relations, school life, leisure time, etc.?
7. Because laymen live on the frontiers of Christian witness, with a variety of gifts for the permeation of all human endeavor, how can they be best prepared for this real task as Christians?
8. Did the Pentecost experience of the early Church (see Acts 2) add any new dimension to the way the Church should see its mission or the way it should pursue it?
9. Do we "in the Church" talk a different language than people "outside" can understand, or start from hidden false assumptions about them, or from an unworthy organizational self-interest, or do we talk too much in terms of negative rules and too little concerning the positive mission? How can we correct these errors?
10. What is the relation of verbal proclamation of the Gospel and the living witness—witnessing by life and word?

THE CHURCH IN THE MISSION OF GOD

3

THE CHURCH IN THE MISSION OF GOD

"The Church (is) . . . in the first place, witness and evidence of that which God has done, and the sign of that which He is doing and will yet do. By this alone the world is apprised of the historical Event and its more-than-historical significance and issues.

"Second, the Church is also the means through which God is carrying His purpose to effect. It is the Body whose members are members of Christ, united with Him and at His disposal. Its life, therefore, is both the extension of His earthly ministry and also a participation of His present and continuing work as risen Lord and Saviour.

"Third, the Church is designed to be the field where the glory of God, once manifested in Jesus Christ to those who had eyes to see, will be revealed to the whole created universe, which meanwhile waits for the manifestation of the sons of God . . .

"It is thus of the very nature of the Church that it has a mission to the whole world. That mission is our participation in the work of God which takes place between the coming of Jesus Christ to inaugurate God's Kingdom on earth, and His coming again in glory to bring that Kingdom to its consummation." ("Christ, the Hope of the World" —Report of the Advisory Commission)

THE MARKS OF THE CHURCH

In the classical Reformation documents there is a standard doctrinal pattern which describes three "marks" by which the true Church is recognized:

a) It is a visible fellowship of believers
b) In which the pure Word of God is preached, and
c) The sacraments are administered according to the ordinances of Christ.[1]

Today there is some strong questioning as to the adequacy of this type of definition; it is suggested that the Reformers' description of the Church was too static, too much a reflection of the medieval setting in which the Church was visualized as local groups in given geographical places doing definite religious acts. The critics insist that the failure of the Reformers to mention *mission* as an essential mark of the Church is a clear failure to be true to the New Testament. In the New Testament there is a passage that does speak as the Reformation definitions do of the three characteristics of the Church (Acts 2:42):

1. They continued in the apostles' teaching (the Word of God)
2. and fellowship
3. in the breaking of bread (sacrament) and the prayers.

---

1. *E.g.,* in Article XIX of the XXXIX Articles of the Anglican Church: "The visible Church of God is a congregation of faithful men in which the pure Word of God is preached, and the sacraments be duly administered according to Christ's ordinance, in all those things that of necessity are requisite to the same." So also Article VII of the Augsburg Confession.

The Reformed family of churches usually lists three marks in their confessional documents:

1) The pure preaching of the Word of God.

2) The right administration of the Sacraments according to the ordinances of Christ.

3) The proper administration of Christian discipline.

But this text is part of the story of Pentecost. There the Apostles are those who are driven out of the upper room, driven by the Holy Spirit out on the path of obedience to the mission given them by Christ—from Jerusalem, to Judea, to Samaria and to the uttermost parts of the earth. To be in the *apostles fellowship* therefore, was to be moving out in mission: a pilgrim people moving out to meet the coming Christ at the ends of time and space, erecting signs of the power of that fellowship to break through the dividing walls of our worldly communities to reveal the unity of life in Christ. But the Reformers failed to include this characteristic of "mission." In fact the strange thing is that they tried to remove it. The commission of Christ to witness from Jerusalem, to Judea, to Samaria and to the uttermost parts of the earth was explained away on the grounds that it was limited to the apostles. This task, they believed, was fulfilled by the apostles. They planted the seeds of the gospel throughout the world, and so the commission ended. Subsequent generations have the task, each in its own place, of seeing that those seeds spread and grow. This is how Luther put it:

> "That the apostles entered strange houses and preached was because they had a command and were for this purpose appointed, called and sent, namely that they should preach everywhere, as Christ had said, 'Go into all the world and preach the gospel to every creature.' After that, however, no one again received such general apostolic command, but every bishop or pastor has his own particular parish."[2]

---

2. So also Calvin: Institutes, Book IV, Ch. 3, paragraphs 4 and 5; and Commentary on I Cor. 12:28.

Would Luther and Calvin oppose "evangelism" and "missions" today? Their evangelical understanding of the faith makes that unlikely. Rather it seems that their struggle against Rome and the political powers of their day meant that they gave no fresh thought to the missionary imperatives. "Christendom" obscured this side

The Reformers thus limited themselves to a "vertical" or "static" view of the church: responsibility for their own place; and so failed to express the "horizontal" or "dynamic" view of the Church which sees it as responsible to move out across the boundaries of space, the boundaries of nation and culture and class, in order to reveal in its life the mission of Christ to gather all things into the unity of his reconciling love.

This view, with consequent missionary failure, was general until the growing mobility of man in the 17th and 18th centuries forced men such as Carey to question these assumptions and to insist that the apostolic mission is essential to the Church for all time. So there was released a new burst of missionary activity. But *were the full consequences of this rediscovery of mission as a central "mark" of the life of the Church worked out in the Church's life?* There is reason to doubt it.

1) Missionary societies were and for the most part still are separate from the center of church life. They are an important, but extra activity.

2) The "vertical" parish view of the church is still the central mental image which dominates our minds; and, as a result, the image of the whole church as a pilgrim body moving out across the dividing walls of nation, race, culture, class is not yet clearly seen and felt.

WHAT MAKES THE CHURCH THE CHURCH?

The need to redefine the "marks of the Church" is clear, if we are to come to a satisfactory understanding of the forms the Church must take if it is to serve the mission of God in the structures of our modern world. More and more writers are insisting that mission is central to the

---

of the truth by leading them to an unexamined acceptance of the assumption that the geographical task of spreading the Gospel was already fulfilled.

true nature of the Church. Often it is said that we must say that "the Church *is* mission"[3] and while others feel that it is going too far to say more than "the Church *has* a mission," there seems to be clear agreement that the Church must reflect its mission in the form of its life.[4]

The big question that now must be faced can be put in this way: "What are the minimum marks of the Church?" or "What are the irreducible characteristics which the

3. Charles D. Kean in his essay "An Anglican Approach to Unity," included in the volume *The Challenge to Reunion,* ed. by R. McAfee Brown and D. H. Scott, gives a characteristic statement of this view. "*The Church is mission.* It does not *have* a mission; it *is* mission. It does not send missionaries; it, itself, is sent. The Church exists not for its own sake but for the sake of the world, and it can never lose sight of this fact without becoming apostate."

4. In the "Report of the Theological Commission on Christ and the Church" (European Section) presented to the Fourth World Conference on Faith and Order at Montreal, July 1963, this statement is given (pp. 49-50, Faith and Order Paper No. 38):

"Through the Holy Spirit the being of the Church is grounded in Christ and his gospel; it is infused with the love of God which has come into the world with Jesus Christ. The essential nature of the Church therefore is agape, the love of God shed abroad in its midst, which the Church must express in its own life. Thus its life is inseparable from its mission. As the Father loves the Son, so the Son loves the Church: as the Son was sent by the Father, so the Church is sent by the Son. The nature and being of the Church are not to be thought of statically but dynamically, in terms of the movement of the divine love from God to men, gathering them into communion with himself. . . .

"God is love, so that as the Church dwells in love, it dwells in God and God in it. In Jesus Christ the love of God was poured out for mankind, and the Church shares in this love. In him this love took the form of a servant and this, too, is the pattern for the Church. The Church follows in the steps of Christ, the Servant of God, not as co-redeemer with him, but that it too may be identified with the world in its sin and guilt, that it may bear it up in prayer and intercession, and spend itself in compassionate sympathy, to the end that all men may be confronted by the Saviour and brought within the active reign of Christ. To fulfill this mission the Church must itself be a fellowship of reconciling love and a fit instrument of that love of God which brought it into existence and determines its inmost being."

Church as an institution must have, if it is to be truly the Church?" One attempt has been made by George Casalis in a paper to the Western European Working Group of the W.C.C. study.[5] Casalis seeks to define the Church from the center of mission. He sees the Church as the servant of God's mission to the world in Christ, and concludes that "for the Bible, the Church appears as a secondary reality. . . . The decisive factor is the relation between the living Lord and humanity." In this same vein Casalis insists that the Church is "a segment of the world which confesses the universal Lordship of Christ; thus it is the place where the world becomes aware of its true destination, its true face (configuration)." Casalis believes that the traditional "marks of the Church"—Word, Sacrament, brotherly love—are usable; but he insists that they should *not* be used as institutional characteristics by which the Church judges her internal life to decide whether she is the Church or not. They *should* be seen as *missionary signs* of the way God brings to the world, *through a piece of itself*, the reality of his reconciling love. In other words, the Church is not given the Word, the Sacraments and brother love for its own internal satisfaction, or for its own separate institutional life; Christ gathers his people, speaks to his people, feeds his people, in order that they bring his reconciling love to the world.

When the Church sees itself as a piece of the world used by God to approach the world which he would redeem, it also is rescued from the temptation to think that God speaks only within the institution of the Church. Knowing that God's purpose enfolds the whole world, and that the Church is a segment of the world which exists for the world, it also knows that God is at work in the rest of the world outside the Church; that he speaks to

5. In the Blue "Concept"—Papers available to members of the Working Groups only.

the world also through pagan witnesses,[6] and that the Church must therefore watch for the signs of God's presence in the world, ready to reach out to work with God at the points where he is at work and to be open to "humble dialogue with pagans."

This attempt to describe the Church in dynamic terms drawn from its role as a servant of God's mission to the world, even to the point of seeing the lines which mark the boundary of the Church's relation to the world dissolve, is one which cuts beneath the unfortunate separations between the Church and the world and forces the Church to seek continually for forms of life which will enable it to maintain situations of dialogue in the world and lines of service within the institutions of the world.

Nevertheless, it is the view of many that we are required by the New Testament to give more definite recognition to the unique characteristics of the life of the Church than this view of Casalis. They believe, moreover, that it is vital to give this more definite statement of the unique "marks" of the true life of the Church, precisely because the characteristics which distinguish it from the world are of vital importance to its mission. These "marks" are signs to the world that the miracles of God's grace already evident (in imperfect form) in the life of the Church, are a foretaste of God's final purpose for the whole of his world. So J. G. Davies claimed that Casalis' view makes "too little of the Church's discontinuity with the world," too little of its own peculiar "givenness" as a separate institutional organ set by God in the world as the sign of his saving purpose.

---

6. Casalis draws attention to the line of pagan witnesses in the Bible from Melchizedek to the rulers of Rom. 13; including Cyrus, the Canaanite women of Mk. 7:24ff, the pagans of Mk. 25:31ff and Rom. 2:14. This line could easily be filled out; and the analysis of the ways in which they are seen as serving God's mission together with the ways in which they are related to the institution of "Israel" old and new, is of great importance for this study of the Church's missionary structure.

Clearly this aspect of the Church's life needs careful examination. If the Church is called to show in its life "given" or unique characteristics which mark the difference between its life and the life of the world (and which therefore are signs to the world of God's purpose for it) then this will make a big difference to the nature of the Church-world dialogue. The forms of the Church's witnessing life will then need to be such that these unique characteristics are clearly expressed.

When we ask, however, what these given "marks" are, the contemporary theological discussion soon pushes us back into deep water. We are forced to recognize that the marks are not "things" that we can control. They are living characteristics of the Church which God gives to her as she is obedient to him in his mission to the world.

When, for example, we speak of "the Word" as a mark of the Church, there is here a responsibility for "right doctrine." Yet, "the Spirit giveth life"; and no amount of care to control the Word can assure the Church of the presence of "the Word truly preached." Only as she risks her inheritance in twentieth century trade—in obedient mission—can she expect the Spirit to give life.

Similarly when we speak of "unity," in one sense this too is capable of control. The New Delhi Assembly was able to state the large measure of agreement among member churches as to the "nature of the unity we seek," and was able to see this as a goal toward which the churches should move with real determination. Nevertheless it is still true that beneath and beyond all external unity is "the unity of the Spirit."

It is sometimes suggested that because this true unity of the Spirit is beyond human control, we should reverse the present concentration upon merger plans which can lead only to external unity, and should first move back within the life of the churches to seek that spiritual renewal from which alone true unity can grow. But the alternative is false. "He that saveth his life shall lose it" applies to church as well as to believer. The church's calling is to offer up her life to the world. She is to seek external unity because her mission requires that the world see in the church the unity promised for all creation. It is in the missionary quest for this unity—a unity that is to be manifested among the disunities of culture, race, class and nation—that the gift of the unity of the Spirit is to be expected.

Here we see the inseparability of *mission* and *unity;* that God gives us the new unity in Christ in order that he may reveal to the world his mission to gather all things into the unity of his life. The ecumenical movement is an expression of the growing recognition in the Church that God is asking us to receive from him the gift of unity in order that we may be truer servants of his mission.[7]

We are being driven to the conclusions that unity is an essential expression of the nature of the Church, and that we are being called (i) to act together now in all areas except where we are prevented by conscientious convictions (at the Lund Faith and Order Conference in 1952 this principle was suggested as an implication of the light God has already given us on the path to unity. It is hardly necessary to state how desperately we are dragging our heels!). (ii) to push on relentlessly to a discovery of the ways in which God is leading us to the dissolution of the remaining barriers of conscientious conviction. (The statement accepted at the Third Assembly at New Delhi concerning the nature of the unity we seek, leaves many un-

7. The Ecumenical Press Service, 11 April 1963, reports this statement from a Situation Conference of the East Asia Christian Conference: "As Christ's mission is one, we dare no longer act as if it is as plural as are our churches and mission agencies." The Conference therefore called for new patterns of Church life in "joint action for mission."

resolved differences of conscientious conviction. But it does represent a major step forward, and surely it is true that God has already shown us enough of his will for us on the way to unity to occupy our present obedience while we are waiting upon him for the further light needed for subsequent steps.)

These conclusions in themselves call for major changes in the missionary structure of the Church, especially when we remember that unity in the Church must be a unity which transcends not only our denominational differences, but also our racial, cultural and economic disunities. "Unity," of course, is one of the traditional marks of the Church. The Nicene Creed speaks of the church as "one, holy, catholic and apostolic." We are being forced to see that this "unity" of the Church must be understood in dynamic terms, and that the unity of the Church's life must be such that it will show how God is breaking through the divisions of the world's structures so that the unity of the Church's life can be a living sign of God's missionary purpose in the world.

MISSION AND UNITY

Unity then is one of the "marks" of the Church; but as we ask how this unity must express itself in the structures of the Church's life, and what other "marks" should be revealed in the Church's life (and how), it is clear that a great deal of work still needs to be done.[8] It is perhaps not

---

8. An important statement of the relation of unity to mission is given in "The Report of the Theological Commission on Christ and the Church" (North American Section), p. 32:

"The Lord again and again recalls his Church to this life for the world. He rebukes the Church for every obstacle placed in the way of his mission. Our divisions, for example, are the negation of that mission. Differences within a subsuming unity or valid diversities may contribute to the health of the body. But real fractures of the Christian community represent a force of evil which militates against

premature, however, to say that there seems to be a clear direction in which the investigation is leading us.

i) *To a redefinition of the traditional Reformation "marks of the Church" by placing them firmly within the framework of the Church's mission.* We have seen that in Acts 2:42 ("they continued in the apostles' teaching and fellowship, in the breaking of bread and the prayers") these characteristics are given within the missionary context of the Pentecost story. As the apostles were driven out of the upper room and set on the road to the uttermost parts of the earth, the life of their fellowship was one in which there was a constant breaking down of the boundaries of the world—nation, race, language, class, culture. The Pentecost story witnesses to the way in which the gift of the Spirit

---

the saving purpose of God. All Christians are therefore under obligation to serve as peacemakers and reconcilers.

"This applies not only to the familiar divisions of churches because of conflicts over matters of faith and order. Churches are also divided by distinctions of social and economic class, by moral conventions, by cultural legacies, by national loyalties, and by racial discrimination or caste exclusiveness. All division in the Church, Christ's chosen instrument of reconciliation and redemption, is evidence that secular attitudes, open or concealed, have been allowed to deflect it from its true mission."

The implications of this for the task of re-structuring the church would seem to be considerable. If we ask how far the Church's present congregational life reflects "secular attitudes" to class, cultural, caste and racial exclusiveness, and then see that the structure of the church's life must reject these divisions in order that the Christian community may reveal to the world the unity of God's saving purpose, we are soon confronted with radical consequences. Similarly, if we ask about "regional" (north and south) or "national" divisions of the Church, we are forced to question whether these prevent the church revealing that unity which witnesses to her mission to show forth the fullness of Christ's reconciling power. The Joint Commission on Church Union in Australia (Congregational, Methodist, Presbyterian) believing that the form of unity should witness to Christ's purpose to transcend distinctions between East and West, white and colored, has recommended a Concordat with the Church of South India as a first step toward that unity. See "The Church: Its Nature, Function and Ordering, together with the Proposed Basis of Union," Melbourne, 1963.

carried the believers into a new unity of common life in Christ across the previously impenetrable barriers of language, religion, race and culture. The life of apostolic fellowship therefore, far from being the self-enclosed life of a new and separate institution in the world, is a life that reveals within the institutional structures of the world a new life that transcends the old walls of division. It is in this way that the Church reveals to the world the new unity of life in Christ.

We are thus brought to see that the "marks of the Church" must be understood as pointing to the missionary purpose of the Church. The pure Word that is to be preached witnesses to Jesus Christ whose mission it is to gather all men into the unity of his life. The pure Word summons the Church to reveal to the world that in the Church's life, the old structural hostilities of the world are being dissolved by the reconciling life of Christ. Similarly the sacraments duly administered are understood as signs of Christ's power to draw believers out of the separations of life in the world into the love and unity of his own redeeming life.

The contemporary investigation seems to be leading us also

ii) To a *recognition of the relationship between the "institutional "marks"* listed in the Reformation documents and in Acts 2:42,[9] and the *"marks" given in the Nicene Creed*

9. The word "institution" has come under attack as a word for the Church. Brunner insists that the Church properly so called is not an institution but "a pure fellowship of persons," and his sympathy for the "no-church" movement in Japan shows how far he is prepared to take his opposition. We are suggesting here that Brunner's distinction does not carry any theological consensus. In the "Report of the Theological Commission on Christ and the Church" (North American Section), pp. 26-30 the viewpoint which seems to express a general consensus is given in the section called "The Church as Event and Institution." The following excerpts are typical:

"Against those who think of structures as absolutized and utterly

("one, holy, catholic and apostolic") which are not "institutional" but are instead descriptions of the distinctive Christian life that should shine through the institutional shapes. It is this latter aspect which is expressed in the

---

inflexible and who find the pattern and presence of Christ and the work of the Spirit wholly and without remainder given in the institution, the rebuke comes, 'where the Spirit of the Lord is, there is freedom' (II Cor. 3:17). For the Bible makes clear that while grace is indeed 'given' to the Church it is never possessed by the Church in the sense of being controlled. The Church lives in the Spirit as the Spirit dwells in it, but the Spirit is God's Spirit and can never become identical with the human spirit nor with the corporate 'spirit' of the empirical Church. . . .

"The Scriptures also warn us against those who, claiming the Spirit's authority as an immediate possession decry all institutional forms or channels. . . . The work of the Spirit is notably marked by richness and variety. . . . But when all this is said, it remains true that in his working the Spirit gives form. As in the Incarnation God binds himself to concrete manhood, so by the Spirit in the Church he works in and through human flesh and blood, words and acts, social and historical structures. Any adequate view of the Church must give proper attention to such social and historical structures.

"Event is never without form. The structured expression of Christ's activity in the Church is not only required by man's historical and social condition. Above all, it is required by the definiteness of the Incarnation, by the enduring identity of the Spirit, and by the fact that in the response men make to Christ in the Spirit they are not extricated from their proper manhood but act in a truly embodied way. Furthermore, the continuity of the event, establishing the consistency of the fellowship of Christian faith, worship and life, can be maintained and has been maintained only in definite patterns. Similarly, the mission of the Church—its apostolicity or 'sentness'—necessitates now as always a structure of mission, a genuine apostolicity, which will guarantee and symbolize the abiding sentness which is integral to its nature."

"Institution," in the sense of "given" continuing characteristics of church life: doctrinal statements, preaching, sacraments, forms of fellowship (no matter how variable the structures) are part and parcel of the necessary witnessing life of the Church. But it is necessary for us to be aware of the tension between "institution" and "event" (see the discussion of this in J. L. Leuba "Institution and Event") in the life of the Church, and constantly to test the institutional shapes to see whether they are serving their missionary purpose of revealing in the world the mission of Christ.

following important passage from the W.C.C.'s document: "A Theological Reflection on the Work of Evangelism."

"What is the meaning of the four marks of the Church in their relation to the servant-ministry of evangelism?

"The Church is One. This is a description of what the Church is, and not an exhortation of what the Church ought to be. God has given oneness to His people and wills to bring all men into the oneness He has given. There is no other name given than the name of Jesus whereby men might be saved. So that in Jesus men find both their own salvation and one another. Here is the ultimate connection between unity and the evangelizing process. The Gospel is proclaimed in order that by it men may be brought into oneness with God and among themselves. Evangelism must carry this credential of unity. It is part of that service of the Church by which men are brought into the unity which God wills and which God has given.

"The Church is Holy. The holiness of the Church is the holiness of its Lord. Men participate in it by the grace of God through the action of the Holy Spirit. That which is holy is that which is set apart for His service. Holiness is the mark of being a servant. This mark belongs to the Church, and evangelism possesses it as a credential.

"The Church is Catholic. It is 'the fulness of Him who fills all in all.' This means that the Church has been given for all men without distinction or exception. It means also that in the Church there is offered to all men in Christ the very fulness of God's grace. Catholicity is the mark of the Church which must lie behind the claim of the evangelist that the Gospel is intended for all men. Where a church is not a home for all, the credential of the evangelist to proclaim the Gospel is compromised.

"The Church is Apostolic. This means that it has been sent by God on a mission in the world and that it has been sent down through the ages in continuity. The evangelist stands in a great succession, and participates in a mission which is itself a part of the continuous action of God in history. The evangelist represents this Apostolic Church to the unbelieving world. Apostolicity is also the Church's eschatological dimension. The mission of the Church is 'until He comes.'"

This agreement (in i and ii) that seems to be emerging, leaves unresolved some of the major questions concerning the Church's institutional life in this "time between the times." In Revelation the Seer is allowed a vision of "the new heaven and the new earth," and he reports "I saw no temple there." This means that the institutional forms adopted in this time are temporary (as are such institutions as the family, the state and economic life). But the question remains as to whether these temporary institutional forms have certain invariable or continuous characteristics (not only doctrine with scripture and sacraments; but are there also fixed forms of ministry and government?) or whether there is great flexibility.

Some writers today are urging that we must be prepared for startling "discontinuity" with the forms of Church life with which we have been familiar for the last 1,000 years or so. They are not suggesting, for the most part, that we need abandon the belief that there is "catholic doctrine" (faith given once-for-all, even though its expression varies from age to age, and even though we have still a long way to go to reach a sufficient level of agreement to allow the catholic character of our faith to be given clear expression). Nor are they suggesting that we can do without the "catholic sacraments" (although again we still are far from agreement concerning their number and meaning for our common life). What they are suggesting is that we must be ready for drastic changes in the ordering of our church's life, and in the way it relates itself to the structures of the world.

C. Ebb Munden, III, writing a review of a series of papers describing experimental forms of new church life, put it this way:

"These papers bear witness not so much to the renewal of the church as to the beginning of the end of the church as we have known it; these papers bear witness to the truth that the possibility of the renewal of the church does not exist apart from the reality of the church's impotence as we have experienced it in our time. In the light of this reality, it would seem to be true that the church today is at the point where we must confess that there is not a continuous line between where we are and the new future. . . .

"Does the church stand today, as is often supposed on the Easter side of the cross? Or . . . does the church stand today before the cross? Is its mission then, to die? Do we affirm the Easter faith in our time by insisting that God raised Jesus from the dead or by daring to risk ourselves in the confidence that God will raise us from the dead? Can we do the former without the latter?

"The possibility to which our own experience and the Holy Scripture and these study papers bear witness is that only as the church dies may it be born again, and only thus will the Word of God become sacramental in the life of the church for the world of our time."[10]

This viewpoint draws on a wide stratum of New Testament texts which speak of dying with Christ, taking up the cross, with the servants not being above their Lord. It draws on texts such as the last judgment parable of Matt. 25 which proclaims that we know Christ only when we move out to serve him on the altar of human need. It takes us into the heart of Philippians 2 where the church is counselled to allow its life to be formed by the attitude of Christ who gave up the security of his privileged status and emptied his life out upon the world even to the extent of becoming a slave to human need and dying for it.

---

10. In "motive," January 1963, reviewing a series of papers issued by the Methodist Student Movement on the subject of the renewal of the Church. (Quoted by permission)

It throws us back upon Paul's statement in Colossians that he fills up what is incomplete in Christ's afflictions on behalf of his Body, the Church.

THE RE-FORMATION OF THE CHURCH

Out of this context, this viewpoint insists that the present structures of the church are so dominated by the church's surrender to its own worldly security, and that the church is so imprisoned within the expensive facades of buildings that relate to men only in a very limited portion of their life, that she can find renewal only as she surrenders these securities and pours herself out upon the world, careless of her own safety or reputation or wealth, allowing *the forms* of her renewed life to grow around all *the shapes of worldly need.* The signs of such renewal are seen by this viewpoint at points of discontinuity with the structures of our present congregational life. The signs of the new shape are seen forming

> around a Yale theological student who goes out to gather together white and negro volunteers to give their summers in a concerted attempt to work amongst those negro students whose hope has died and whose despair is revealed in their academic failure, their drop out from school, and their unemployed status;
> around those who struggle amidst hatred, fear and persecution to find new forms of integrated life across the terrible barrier of race conflict;
> around worker priests, unsupported by and even thrust out by the church authorities;
> around a dialogue situation with the world in coffee shops;
> around small Christian groups involved in renewal action in the tragic areas of urban life—with narcotics, or in political action or urban renewal;
> around small "koinonia" groups gathered together to wrestle

with the problems of their vocational life and their *being* the church in their work of the world;

around a lay training center seeking for forms of witness in the areas of modern culture lost to the church.

Such new forms of life have only tenuous connections with the present congregational structure; and to some critics it even seems that we cannot hope for a direct transition from our present congregational pattern to the new shapes the church's life must take.

It would be senseless to minimize the conflict that is coming at this point.[11] Instead we must do our utmost to see the dimensions of the issue and to seek for a theological approach which will help us to see where we should go. It is clear, for example, that even if the *negative judgment* of these critics is wrong and there is no need to think of the drastic death of our present congregations and of violent discontinuity, their *positive concern* must still be recognized. They see the New Testament as witnessing to a Church which *takes form in the world in response to the structures of the world's need.* They see the "means of grace"—word, sacraments, fellowship, ministries—as Christ's gifts to his people to equip us for service in the world of need. They see, therefore, that if the present patterns of congregational life are inadequate to reach out to the drastically altered shape of modern need,[12] then it is idolatry

---

11. It is felt in every part of the Church including Rome where the worker priest problem was a point of direct conflict, but men like Hans Kung and Yves Congar are pressing for structural changes to free the church for direct missionary engagement in the structures of life where the laity must carry on the mission of the church.

12. Hans Margull expresses this by saying that "the structures of our congregations have become designed almost exclusively for people to 'come' and not also for people to 'go.' 'Going' has become a separate function, with 'coming' being the norm." This "come structure" is largely responsible, Margull says, for the truth of the observation of the Central Committee of the W.C.C. at its meeting at Rolle in 1951:

(worshipping a thing for its own sake) to continue a thought-habit which leads us to see the church from the center of a particular structure—local church, building, clergy, congregational worship, committees—and which does not give the freedom to see the church as the love of Christ taking form in the world in response to the call of worldly need.

If we are to ask *how* the church should take form round these worldly needs, however, we must ask again what is essential to the church's life: what is continuous; what can change? Here we can conveniently begin with a traditional distinction between the "instituted" or "given" means of grace and the "prudential" or "flexible" means of grace.

INSTITUTED AND PRUDENTIAL MEANS OF GRACE

John Wesley distinguished the "instituted" from the "prudential" means of grace by describing the former as those instituted by Christ as unchangeable characteristics of the Christian community—such as prayer (public and private), searching the scriptures, attendance upon the sacraments, fasting and "Christian conference"—and by describing the "prudential" means of grace as the changing structures of

---

> "The average congregation is apt to be an introverted community which does not think primarily of its obligation to bring the knowledge of Christ to its whole neighborhood and to the whole world, and this introversion is apt to mark the life, thought and leadership of the whole Church. This applies to the younger Churches as well as to the older.
>
> "Even where the obligation is acknowledged and acted upon, such actions tend to take the form of a separate 'mission' supported by the congregation but not regarded as the responsibility of every member."

Margull concludes that "attempts to strengthen our congregations spiritually will be possible and effective only where the whole structure of the congregation is designed in such a way as to show that for Christians to come obviously means also to go: A Christian grows in participation in God's work in the world."

the Christian life needed to relate it to the changing circumstances of the world.[13] Wesley saw his own "Societies" as an expression of prudential means of grace which he struggled to keep within the Church of England, believing that in the life of the Church the continuity of the "instituted" means of grace was given. But he believed that his societies were vital to the mission of the Church because they provided for the necessary "prudential" forms in which the changeless life of the Church could be brought to men in the changing circumstances of their life.

For example, the parish Church could provide for regular worship, with public prayer, exposition of scripture and administration of the sacraments. But Wesley believed that *ecclesiolae in ecclesia*—small churches within the "great congregation"—were necessary to provide for the mutual care and training of converts for their Christian life in the context of the emerging town life of the eighteenth century. He therefore developed his "class meetings," provided the members with definite disciplines, and produced "rules" which would help the converts to discover a "style of life" that was relevant to their eighteenth century existence.

This distinction between "instituted" and "prudential" means of grace would seem to be useful to guide us in our attempt to evaluate the experiments which today are trying to discover the forms of church life that will express the Church's mission. The stress on "instituted" means is a warning against any restructuring which threatens to jettison those means of grace given to the Church by Christ as permanent and essential characteristics of her life. This we have already discussed in connection with the "marks of the Church." Now the stress on "prudential" means takes us a step further by reminding us that the Church must always develop forms of life which will provide the ways by which these "means of grace" may produce a Christian

13. John Wesley, Works VIII, p. 322-324.

style of life as the believers participate in the particular structures of the life of their own age. The "prudential means of grace" are changeable, because they must be related to the changing needs of the time; but *they are not optional.* A living Church must be seeking for the forms of life which will provide for the presence of Christ with his people at the particular places where the life of their time calls forth a particular form of Christian obedience.[14]

In this context we can understand some of the major movements that are agitating the Church at present, and can see their interrelation:[15]

---

14. "The Report of the Theological Commission on Christ and the Church" (North American Section) p. 24 makes this point from a different angle:

"As the incarnate Son was truly man, so is the Church wrought out of the stuff of human existence. The Church is shaped in and out of the realities of human historicity and sociality. Therefore the Church is not some 'ideal' community, existing in airy abstraction from the affairs of men. Neither is it 'spiritual' in the sense that it is to be contrasted with the hard and inevitable materialities of that world of history and sociality. To call the Church ideal or spiritual in those senses is to fall into ecclesiological docetism akin to the ancient heresy which denied to our Lord his physical body, his historical actuality, his immersion in the stuff of common life. We protest against every view of the Church which in a mistaken effort to exalt its nature as the body of Christ, succeeds only in making it 'purer' than its Lord.

"In obedience to Christ and the Spirit, as the event of their presence and as properly patterned after Christ himself, the Church is necessarily in, as well as with and for the world. It stands in and with the world as testifying to an act of God's gracious calling, a decision and determination which apply not alone to the members of this community, but to the whole of humanity and to every individual within that whole. The Church stands in and with the world by its mission, by its taking the world to itself as the object of its love and concern, by identifying itself with the world as Christ identified himself with sinful humanity. It stands in and for the world as representing the whole of mankind in its praise, its thanksgiving, its confession, its petition, and also in its penitence and constant seeking for forgiveness. The Church's life before God is not a life for itself, but for the world."

15. These movements are inter-related not only in the sense that

a) *The liturgical movement* represents the need to discover forms of worship which express the "instituted" character of the church's life in her unchanging dependence upon the "given" story of redemption and the continuing apostolic life; and the "prudential" character, which relates this "given" life to the language, music, action and needs of contemporary life.

b) The struggle over *Biblical interpretation* which centers upon the need to translate the "given" gospel into the changed thought forms of the present.

c) The concern with the church's *"missionary structures,"* and the attempts to discover the forms of "congregational" or "gathered" life which will continue to express the "given" or "continuous" aspects of the church's life, but will relate these to the structures of our present society in such a way that they express and serve the mission of Christ.

In this third area, which is our particular concern, we ask then what are the characteristics of the "prudential" forms of life? The first answer is that they must relate the "instituted" means of grace to the structured forms of present need.

KOINONIA GROUPS

At present there are signs of a widespread use of *"ecclesiolae"* which may serve the essential purpose of being

---

they all express the same tension between "event" and "institution" and between the "given" and the "contingent"; but also in the sense that the study of one of them is inevitably related to the study of the others. This study on "The Missionary Structure of the Congregation" is therefore inextricably interwoven with the studies in the areas (a) and (b) being carried on by the Faith and Order Commissions of the W.C.C. It is for this reason that liberal use is made of these in the footnotes and it is encouraging that these separate studies in the other areas seem to be pointing to conclusions similar to those that are beginning to emerge in this study.

instruments for relating the Christian life to the major corporate structures of our modern life; thereby allowing a Christian style of life to emerge at these points. One name by which such groups are commonly called is "Koinonia groups"[16]; a name which expresses their central feature—the "sharing" within a small group of a mutual concern for each other's growth within a common dependence upon the gifts of the Holy Spirit. The criterion which we suggested for prudential means of grace—that they should relate the instituted means of grace to the structured forms of present need—would seem to be the basic presupposition of these groups. To point the moral we now need to draw out the implications of this dual characteristic:

1) *Applying the instituted means of grace.* That there is still disagreement at this point is clear—for example, over the place of sacraments and over the relation between ordained and lay ministries in the process of mutual edification. Nevertheless there is sufficient agreement for us to say that major foci of the life of these groups will be

a) Bible study
b) Prayer
c) Sacramental life
d) Concern with some "worldly" problem with which they are related in their daily life in the world
e) The acceptance of some form of *common discipline* and *mutual responsibility*.

In "The Renewal of the Church,"[17] Visser 't Hooft shows that a common component of all the renewal movements down through the history of the Church has been an emphasis upon confrontation with the Biblical message—a dialogue of God's people with "the Word of God" in the

---

16. See a good description of one form of these groups in Robert A. Raines "New Life in the Church," Harper and Row.

17. W. A. Visser 't Hooft, "The Renewal of the Church," p. 90-95.

context of a dialogue with each other. In this free interpersonal relationship of the ecclesiolae; the waiting upon the truth that the Holy Spirit brings to his people through the Word and the readiness to hear what this offers and demands in life today; there lies the first secret that opens the way to renewal. It is within the life of a small group sharing insight that this path to growth into Christ is most likely to be discovered.

Similarly it should be axiomatic for Christians that it is only in the attitude of common dependence upon God in prayer, and only in the attitude of common responsibility for each other in prayer, that the Spirit feeds his people with those gifts of grace by which they are fitted for the service of Christ in the world. J. E. Skoglund goes so far as to say:

> "The potential (for Church renewal) lies not in better organization, more authority, greater promotion, a better educated clergy, or a more literate laity. They have their place, but they are not primary. Power, the kind of power the church can use to fulfil its God-given mission, comes only through waiting and prayer. Only when the church through the centuries has rediscovered this has the church made its mark upon the world. Only as the church of today rediscovers this, will it be able to speak a definite word to the world in revolution. Let the church wait and pray until God gives the Spirit. Then there will be power to witness. The church will then have found its mission in being caught up in the Spirit's mission to the world."[18]

This waiting upon God in prayer, both Scripture and experience teach, is most fruitfully fulfilled in the life of small groups of mutual care and concern where the members facing common problems learn to "bear one another's burdens and so fulfil the law of Christ." Since the center of the Christian life is the way of love, it is in fellowship

---

18. J. E. Skoglund, "To The Whole Creation," The Judson Press, pp. 89-90. (Quoted by permission)

of those who are together learning this way that "growth in grace" most naturally occurs.

It must be added that there is a strong current of witness in the church which says that this waiting upon God has been given a definite shape, and that the life of *ecclesiolae* should be seen as participating within the larger framework of the *liturgy* of the *ecclesia,* with both small group worship and personal worship being seen as a continuation and extension of the worship of the whole Body of Christ. This worship has been given by God a definite shape—the liturgy is a re-enactment of and participation in the shape of God's saving action—and it is as our lives are taken up into this shape that we are prepared for our mission in the world. R. H. Fuller[19] speaks of "the liturgy as the mainspring of evangelism. . . . The church, by being the church in the liturgy ("being the church" rather than "going to church" is a slogan of the liturgical movement) exhibits forth what the gospel really means: the mighty act of God in Christ by which sinful, fragmented humanity is integrated into the body of Christ and the fellowship of the Spirit."

It must be emphasized, of course, that this is true only when the shape of the liturgy is allowed to work itself out into the shape of the life of God's people in the world. Fuller recognizes that:

> "Those who partake of the one bread and are cemented into the one body go out into the world, and what if they return to a world in which they are divided by race and class? They are surely eating the bread and drinking the wine to their own condemnation and are guilty of the body and blood of Christ, if they sit down complacently

---

19. R. H. Fuller "Liturgy and Devotion," in "The Place of Bonhoeffer," edited by Martin E. Marty, Association Press, 1962, pp. 167-194. (Quoted by permission)

> and acquiesce in the injustices which deny what they are, one body, one humanity reintegrated in a common Head."

It can be added that in the small group which sees its life as the extension of the sacramental presence of Christ, the believers see their life being shaped by the action of Christ in his unconditional giving of himself "for others"; and they see their group life as stirring one another up through mutual care and encouragement to fulfil their mission of a life of self-giving for others in the world. To bring to the participants this implication of the liturgy, there is a widespread acceptance of such reforms as the bringing of "the altar" down into the midst of the people; the re-introduction of the "Great Entrance" with representative laymen bringing in the bread and wine as symbols of the need to bring the "things" of daily life that they may be transformed by the shape of Christ's self-giving; and the opening of the liturgy to the expression of the present concerns, problems and tasks of the people[20] so that our self-offering will include our responsibilities, and the self we receive back from Christ will be the self-in-community with its mission set within the particular tasks to which Christ appoints us in the world.

2) All this should make it clear that as we speak about "applying the instituted means of grace" we should speak at the same time of applying them *to the structured forms of present need*. The *Koinonia groups* are today the promise of renewal, but there is danger that they will fail in their purpose because of a failure of relation to the world and its needs. Gordon Cosby of "The Church of the Savior" in Washington, has said that in the small groups that were centered around Bible study, prayer and mutual care, there was for a time a most encouraging evidence of personal renewal. After some time however, there was a

20. See the way this occurs in the East Harlem Protestant Parish, as reported in G. W. Webber "God's Colony in Man's World," Abingdon.

discouraging dissipation of spiritual energy. Not until the groups were reformed, and became mission groups, taking their shape from a particular need in the world where the members of the group felt a common call to witness and service, did the groups recover their life and growth.[21]

Here we are at the heart of the problem of "missionary structure." The implication would seem to be that groups of Christians must be drawn into the various structures of the world, revealing in the shape of their corporate life the redeeming power and purpose of Christ. Archie Hargreaves in his booklet "Stop pussyfooting through a revolution. Some churches that did," tells the story of several churches that allowed themselves to have their congregational life radically reshaped by discovering the shapes of need in their community, and being ready to be reshaped around those needs. These examples merit close study. But the major question is this: Can the local residence congregation serve as an adequate form for this movement out into the structures of the world's need?

The examples given in Hargreaves booklet are evidence that a lot can be done from this point. But there would seem also to be ample evidence that the local residence congregation is not the suitable form for moving out to many of the needs of our modern world. The experience of the home mission societies over the last century would seem to indicate that there are major needs that local congregations cannot meet—migrant workers, for example, and institutions such as hospitals and universities. Similarly the rise of "Evangelical Academies" or "Church and World Institutes" in Europe, or a Detroit Industrial Mission, would

21. This story of The Church of the Savior written by Gordon Cosby's secretary, Elizabeth O'Connor, is most instructive. The key to the story is clearly in the readiness to allow the life of the believers to be drawn out to the world's needs while maintaining firm hold on "the means of grace." The book is called: "The Call To Commitment," Harper and Row.

seem to indicate that if the Christian mission is to be fulfilled in those sociological strata that are separated from local residence communities—industrial life, political life, intellectual communities, the world of art, mass media—then *groups* must emerge which find their Christian mission in relating the gospel to those areas of life. So far, even where these developments have occurred, there is a tendency to look upon the resultant forms as "secondary," with the local residence congregation as "normal" or "primary." Is this justified? Or should we now be prepared to see the church taking form in the various aspects of our world—residential, industrial, educational, political, cultural—with each of these being an expression of the mission of Christ to bring all aspects of life under his Lordship? And, if so, how can these various aspects then be related to each other so that the life of the church can give expression to the mission of Christ to bring all of life into the unity of his one life?

QUESTIONS

1. What makes the church the Church?
2. How can individual members—or "membranes"—of the body of Christ maintain vital relationship with the Head and with other members of the body?
3. What are some of the better ways to maintain "dialogue" with "the world"? How can we be agents of gospel confrontation of persons, and "areas of the world's life" that need such confrontation?

4. If God has given his Church unity and mission, why are we so often unaware of these gifts and failing to appropriate them?
5. Do these gifts of mission and unity comprehend more than just "task" and "togetherness"?
6. In how far is the church flexible and open to develop new forms of life and means of expression to meet today's developing needs in the world?
7. As the Church experimentally develops new forms of life ("ecclesiolae" or "koinonia" groups) around the problems and needs of the world, how can these "groups" be brought together in the total congregational pattern ("ecclesia"), and not "written off" as unrelated or "outside the Church"?

THE CHURCH IN THE WORLD

4

THE CHURCH IN THE WORLD

The task of this final chapter is to explore some of the possibilities that lie in the suggestion that the Church must "let the world write the agenda" if it is to be truly the servant of God's mission in today's alienated and fragmented society—or, to put it another way, we must explore the thesis that the time has come to allow the Church to take shape around the needs of the world.

In the previous chapters it has become clear that if we are to follow this way there are certain theological requirements that must be met. For example, as the Church takes changing form it must still reveal those "marks" which witness to its "givenness"—to the fact that it is the possession of Christ; that it can continue to be the Church only as it lives "in the apostles' fellowship"; that it is called to stand forth in the midst of the broken world as a "sign" of God's purpose to redeem the world.

When we say therefore, that "the world must be allowed to write the agenda," it quickly appears that there is a necessary limitation to what we mean by agenda. The limitation is properly expressed by the Orthodox theologian, Father Schmemann, when he insists that the Church is not a democracy, for "she is governed not by the people and for the people—but by God and for the fulfilment of His Kingdom. Her structure, dogma, liturgy and ethics do not depend on majority vote, for all these elements are God given and God defined."[1] Nevertheless, the possibility for letting the world write the agenda, lies in the way God has given himself in Christ: as the servant, who allowed himself to take form within the forms of human need, humbling himself and becoming obedient to the world's demand; even unto death (Phil. 2).

CHRIST IS LORD—OVER WORLD AND CHURCH

In examining the possibilities for the re-formation of the Church around the structures of the world's needs, we run quickly into a major theological issue concerning the nature of the church-world relationship. Professor Casalis raised the issue at the first meeting of the Western European Working Group when he said that in the Church we have developed the habit of thinking in the order *God-Church-World,* whereas the Biblical witness should lead us to think the other way around: *God-World-Church.* God is not concerned first with the Church; and we should not think of the Church as God's sole partner, with God and the Church directing their action at the world. God is first concerned with the world (Casalis insists); it is there that he is at work working out *his purpose for the world.* The Church is simply a part of the world—the part which is aware of Christ's Lordship over the world, and so is ready to recognize what God is doing in the world and to join him in that action.

---

1. Father Schmemann, "Clergy and Laity in the Orthodox Church." To some extent, of course, the "God given" and "God defined" structure, dogma, liturgy and ethics all must take on changing form in new circumstances. There are areas of church life, also, where democracy can properly be allowed to operate. But the point is that restatements of "God given" dogma, are brought to the church as the Holy Spirit gives new understanding of the truth given in Christ, and the true guidance of the fellowship is a gift "from above" by the Holy Spirit, not a democratic sharing of human insight "from below."

There has been a good deal of resistance to the way in which Casalis has stated the issue. In part the resistance is due to the feeling that Casalis understates the particular character of Christ's relation to the Church—a unique relation which sets the Church apart as a witness to and foretaste of God's redeeming work. But even if it should be agreed that Casalis has failed to give adequate expression to the unique character of the Church as an institution, he still raises the all-important question as to whether the Church, in all its uniqueness, is meant as a "sign" of God's purpose for the whole world; and whether the Church therefore exists *for* the world.

Gibson Winter raises one of the major aspects of this question in a discussion of "piety" and "servanthood" as motifs for the life of the Church.[2] *"Pietism"* describes the Church when it is preoccupied with private values—such as emotional balance, the nurture of children and the development of personal moral virtues; with a concentration upon the home. "Servanthood" describes the Church when it sees its responsibility as ministering to the total life of the "metropolis"; preparing the laity to witness, within the structures of society, to the destiny of *the world* in the final purpose of God.

In contrasting the two motifs, Winter is careful to say that he does not mean that pietism should be discarded as a needed symbol of Christian life. Instead, he is saying that "servanthood" should be the primary motif; and it is only when this true order is kept that a true piety appears.

> "Every image of the Church involves an appropriate kind of piety, a corresponding personal devotion and exercise in the Christian life. This subjective side of the historical existence of the Church is integral to Christianity; indeed, personal devotion and discipline have always

2. Gibson Winter, "The New Creation as Metropolis," MacMillan, 1963, Chapter I. (Quoted by permission)

played a significant part in the total life and witness of the churches.

"When servanthood is contrasted with pietism in the present day, the contrast is between churches that are engaged in the metropolitan struggle through witnessing laity and churches that are insulated from the public struggle and preoccupied with the private values of residential community. There will be a piety appropriate to the servanthood of the laity in the metroplis, but it will be a very different kind of piety from that of the medieval churches or the frontier towns."[3]

This helps us to see the symbolic value of Casalis' reversal of the order of relationship. It could be misleading if it resulted in a depreciation of the importance of the Church as a "place" where Christian life receives its meaning and identity. It could be valid if it is saying that the meaning the Church gives to Christian lives is that it makes visible their servant character in the world, revealing Christians as those who are conscious of Christ's Lordship over the world and who therefore see themselves placed in the world at the disposal of Christ's Lordship.

Winter expresses this valid meaning of the reversal of order in the following statement:

"In the servant Church, ministry is servanthood within the world. Ministry is discerning the promise of the saving history in the historical decisions of public responsibility;

3. *Ibid.*, pp. 20-21. Winter also gives an important warning against a dangerous misunderstanding that could easily arise at this point.

"To defend piety as an important aspect of the Church's life is not to propose that our immediate task is to cultivate a piety appropriate to metropolis. This is the mistake of most of the renewal movements in the churches. True piety emerges in the engagement of the Church with the world. *True piety is the subjective expression of the objective ministry of the Church in the world.* Only as the churches become the servanthood of the laity in the metropolitan areas will a piety emerge which is appropriate to metropolis. The Christian style of life is not the means to engagement in the world but the consequence of a ministry in the world." (p. 25.)

> ministry is also discerning the truly human in the spheres of personal association and family life. In a secularized world, ministry is realized in the decisions for a responsible society. . . . Those who are especially ordained for sacramental celebration also have ministries in the servant Church, but their ministry is to equip the Church in its witness and servanthood in the world. This shift in the character of ministry can be dramatized thus: the ministry is usually conceived today as the work of clergymen with auxiliary aids among the laity; ministry in the servant Church is the work of laity in the world with auxiliary help from theological specialists."[4]

What is at stake here, is not the order of the words, God-world-church. In one sense the last two words can have no order, for they are inter-related aspects of the one Lordship of Christ. The significance of the change of order by Casalis is that it is a symbolic call for a change in the dominant attitude of the Church's present relation to the world. He is insisting that what is needed is a rediscovery of the meaning of the servant role in the Church's relation to the world.

We can contrast the two attitudes to the relation of the Church to the world by the example of two ways often implicit in the relation of the Church to the state:

a) *Pietist.* The unconscious (even conscious) belief that the role of the State must be to serve the Church—either by enacting the churches' (usually restrictive) moral legislation, or by giving advantaged status to the churches (by sabbath laws or tax benefits). The state's role is seen as directly helping the Church by training citizens in the Church's moral way of life, and (at least indirectly) helping the Church to gather everybody in.

b) *Servant.* The belief that the state has its God-given ministries—such as keeping order, justice, peace and serving

4. *Ibid.,* p. 59.

Christ's ultimate purpose of bringing the whole creation to unity in him—and that the role of the Church is to train the laity for service in these ministries within the State.

THE MINISTRIES OF THE CHURCH

The relation of the Church to the world comes to focus in the question of the ministry of the "laos" in relation to the ministry of the "ordained." The concentrated attention given to this question in recent literature[5] has revealed that in the New Testament all members of the laos have ministries and that the role of special ministries ("ordained") within the Church is to "equip the saints for the work of ministry." Father Schmemann expresses the "inner-Church" relation as follows:

> "There is no opposition between clergy and laity in the Church. Both are essential. The Church as a totality is Laity; and the Church as a totality is Inheritance, the Clergy of God. And in order to be this, there must exist within the Church, the distinction of functions, of ministries that complete one another. The clergy are ordained to make the Church the gift of God—the manifestation and communication of His truth, grace and salvation to men. It is their sacred function, and they fulfill it only in complete obedience to God. The laity are ordained to make the Church the acceptance of that gift, the 'Amen' of mankind to God. They equally can fulfill their function only in complete obedience to God. It is the same obedience: to God and to the Church, that establishes the harmony between clergy and laity, makes them one body growing into the fulness of Christ."[6]

---

5. Father Yves Congar, "Laity, Church and World," Helicon; H. Kraemer, "A Theology of the Laity," Westminster Press; Francis O. Ayres, "The Ministry of the Laity," are representative works among this literature. The Bulletins of the Department of the Laity of the W.C.C. contain a wealth of material on the subject.

6. Father Schmemann, *op. cit.*

A further question however is: what are the lay ministries *in the world?* Certainly they have their "gathered" or "inner" significance in the mutual edification of each other in the Body of Christ through the sharing of spiritual gifts. If, however, the Church exists for the world, and if Christians are given secular ministries within the institutions of the world—such as home, state, work—a fact which many ethical passages of the New Testament make clear (e.g., Rom. 13:1-2; I Tim. 2:1-7; I Peter 2:13-3:18.), then the "scattered" or "servant" life of the Church should be the major focus of ministry. The inner exists to equip us for the outer.

It can scarcely be denied that all too often the rediscovery of the ministry of the laity has been short-circuited at the point of the "inner." Laity have been recruited to do more inside the Church; but the only result (all too often) has been to turn them into clericalized laymen. By concentrating their energies inside the Church the vision of their lay ministries in the world has been lost. This is what Winter means by a Pietist Church; whereas a Servant Church would see the inward ministry as equipping the saints for their ministries in the world.[7]

7. The need for the development of lay ministries in the world has given rise to experiments with "worker priests." Insofar as these represent an attempt to relate the "ordained" ministry to the structures of the world they may serve a vital role in symbolizing the proper concern of the church with these structures. The ultimate need however, is for the ordained to serve their role in helping to train the laity for these ministries. It seems logical to expect that this will entail special ministries to serve this purpose. This belief lies behind the proposal for a contemporary diaconate in the "Second Report of the Joint Commission on Church Union" in Australia:

> "Deacons" have normally been those designated for the exercise of the Church's ministry of service to the world—the care of the poor, the sick and others in need—although sometimes the office has been narrowed by becoming predominantly concerned with the property and finance of the congregation.
>
> "We believe that the important insight represented by the Reformed office of ordained elders is that it takes into the oversight of

A further step is now needed. If the gathered Church trains the laity for their ministries in the scattered world of secular institutions, *it would seem logical that the gathering itself should be at places which are appropriate for training the laity for their scattered life.* This brings us back to the expressed doubt that the Church can fulfill its total mission in the world through a congregational life that is related primarily to only one aspect of the world's existence—residence. As we saw in Chapter 1, when the residence congregation arose, all the major aspects of life were then related to residence. Now residence is an isolated island in the mobile society of modern urban life.

HERETICAL STRUCTURES

The Western European Working Group raised the question as to whether it is justified to speak of "heretical structures."[8] We speak of "heretical doctrines" as those which distort the truth of God's relation to us and to the world. Can we also speak of "heretical structures" as those which

---

the congregation representative laity who are involved in the vocations of the world, and symbolizes also the reaching out of the ministry of the Church into the secular occupations of everyday life. The time of Union provides an opportunity for a creative re-interpretation and broadening of this valuable form of the ministry, so that members of the laity can be admitted to the diaconate, participating with the presbyters in the oversight of the congregation, and also reaching out into the ordinary vocations of life there to exercise their ministry of oversight and leadership among their fellow Christians in the world."

The proposal by Bishop Newbigin for a greater use of "non-professional ministers" who will earn their living in ordinary occupations, but will also serve as ministers of the Word and Sacraments, could fulfil the same purpose; particularly in rural and small town settings.

8. The term was used informally in the meeting of the Western European Working Group by the Roman Catholic sociologist Dr. Greinacher. After preliminary discussion in that meeting, it was taken up by the Working Group in East Germany and is now receiving widespread attention.

are not fitted to express God's true relation to the present world? Their tentative answer was that this term is justified and that "structures are heretical if they belittle God's mission or action."

This conclusion could be supported from passages such as Matt. 25:31-46 cf. Matt. 5:23-24. If Church structures train believers only to practice the presence of Christ within the Christian community; and therefore fail to train them to recognize Christ's presence at the points of worldly need and to serve Christ on *that* altar; then those structures are heretical.

The Western European Working Group arrived at this conclusion:

> "A preliminary answer to this difficult question might be the following: Heretical structures are structures which prevent the Gospel from reaching its intended goal. In other words, structures are heretical when they prevent the congregation from penetrating into every geographic and social realm, thus standing between the Gospel and the world."

The East German Group gave it as their witness that in the environment where they are called to serve, external pressure has brought about the collapse of a series of heretical structures—structures of an introverted church that was oblivious to the needs of the world. It is their experience that they are being called now to re-form in small Christian brotherhoods in direct response to the needs of their world for Christian witness and service.

This brings us to the vital question: What are the forms that will direct the life of the Church to its intended goal of penetrating "every geographic and social realm"? On what basis can the Church decide what are the appropriate gathering points? "The Missionary Task of the Church: Theological Reflections," approached the question in this way:

"The Church is sent into the world, in order to gather men from every nation into the one household of God. . . . It is an essential part of the strategy of mission for the Church to identify itself with men in their separate 'groupings,' in such a way that the Christian faith takes form within the particular cultural forms of their daily life. . . . The mission of the Church requires both that measure of identification with men in their groupings which enables them to hear the Word of God in their 'own tongue,' to worship God within their own world of symbol and emotions, and to discover the way of obedience to Christ within the peculiarities of their own life, and also that measure of transcendence over the barriers that divide groups of men from each other, which will witness to the power of Christ to unite all things in one in Him."

In the Working Groups only preliminary attempts have been made to identify the most important "structures" of the world that may call for "gathering." The following list therefore, is highly tentative and is given simply to illustrate the direction of the investigation.

1. *Direct sociological structures* giving rise to continuing institutions—such as political structures, businesses, vocational groups, communications and entertainment media, educational and health institutions.

2. *Communities of concern* (e.g., the "world" of the arts) and *communities of need* (e.g., drug addicts). Unlike the first group these are not so much organized institutions as changing communities gathering around the concerns and needs.

3. *Major social crises* necessitating structured responses —e.g., race, housing, poverty, war.[9]

9. The nature of these structures varies greatly. Those in 1. are continuing structures: this area corresponds to the traditional "orders" or "mandates" of Christian social ethics. Even here however, continuity of structure is associated with wide changes within those structures. When we move to 2. and 3., the measure of visible structural continuity diminishes, although the categories remain. (Continued)

By taking examples, from each of these groups, of ways in which churches are seeking to develop forms of life through which to express their servant ministries, we will attempt to discuss this problem of what are "true" and what are "heretical" structures. To help in the discussion we will make continued reference back to the theological issues raised in the previous chapters.

A preliminary question, however, requires our attention: If we seek to develop forms of Church life within these structures of the world, *what should be the basic characteristic of the church-world relationship?* Are we there primarily as informants (how can they hear without a speaker?) or as servants (that they may see your good works)?

Eberhard Müller describes the relationship which must develop as one of "dialogue"—one in which the church listens to the concerns of the world; gets to know its questions, its concerns, its needs; and then identifies itself with these concerns in such a way that the Christian with his worldly brother reaches out to Christ to discover what his Lordship means in that particular area of life.

> "God speaks to men and he commands us to do the same with our fellowmen. Man is called to be God's partner. We subtly reject this gracious relationship if we are not prepared to accept our human brother as our partner. The aim of discussion is mutual understanding. Understanding means that I am received and listened to by the other man and he is received and listened to by me. In the relationship which God has chosen with me this is similarly true. So as Christians we must not enter upon a debate that aims at making the other silent. We must remain open for the other man's true insight into reality and the ideas

---

This variability in continuity and change factors is obviously significant in any attempt to develop witnessing forms of the church in these areas. Particularly there will be need to guard against the tendency to build "permanent" structures to relate the life of the church to structures that are undergoing radical change.

> that he has developed in serious responsibility before the truth. Those who fanatically fight for principles are always men of monologue."[10]

Müller insists that *true dialogue is with persons in their present sociological settings.* He describes the needed dialogue as one in which "the truth of God and the world of modern technology are brought together in meaningful conversation." What needs renewal, he claims, is "not so much the Church itself as the Church's mission to the world."[11] Müller suggests as steps in this dialogue:

---

10. In a Methodist Student Movement pamphlet: "The German Evangelical Academies and Church Renewal," by Dr. Eberhard Müller.

11. This sentence seems to reflect the tendency still to think of "church" as a *base* located in the residential community from which the church sets out on mission. Is this justified? If the church's mission to the world is renewed, is not the church renewed so that it is present in the world at the point of mission? Dr. Müller speaks in the pamphlet of the communities outside the residential congregation as "para parishes"; and even goes so far as to say that "the congregation in the full sense of the term is only possible where people live. Therefore the local parish will always be the center of the Church." Is not this an illustration of the enslavement of our thinking by the traditional (medieval) residence parish? Is it not true, for example, that in large measure people no longer live where they reside, and that therefore the church has to take form around their life at the points where the major concerns of their existence find expression?

Dr. Müller's conclusion is that the "Church must form, besides the local parish, mobile service groups, and send them out into the fields of the modern world." The structures he suggests are: 1. *Service groups* in such fields as industry, agriculture, crafts, administration and politics, health, education, mass media, traffic and tourism, cultural services. 2. *Regional centers* to train people for these service groups. 3. *The suburban parish* as the basic unit of church life.

Is it not possible that residence should be seen with the other sociological forms requiring "service groups"? And would it not perhaps be more accurate to speak of all these as "ecclesiolae" reaching out into particular areas and still leaving the church with the necessity of developing forms of life which will witness to Christ's power to reunite that which the world divides. For this role the suburban parish cannot be the basic unit; for in residence communities there has developed radical segregation on cultural class and racial lines. The "basic unit" of church life will need to witness more directly to the New Creation.

a) *Encounter*—"encounter in equality" with the groups of the world; usually in a "reconstructed" community of the world since it is normally not possible at first to meet with these groups in their working setting.

b) *Reflection*—bringing together Christians and those who want to cooperate with them; in factories, offices and professional organizations; and nurturing this nucleus as a continuing community.

This insistence of Müller upon "dialogue" as the form of the Church's relation to the structures of the world has a double merit. On one side it underlines the truth that our Christian concern with men in these structures of the world is not simply a tactic for gaining the interest of non-Christians so that we may then slip in our Christian witness. Our concern with these structures is genuine because we know that they have their role to play in God's mission, and that Christians must therefore learn how to fulfil their ministry in those structures while seeking to bring their fellowmen to an awareness of their God-given function. On the other side, the emphasis on "dialogue" also is a call to the Church to confess the measure of our alienation from the world and of our need to listen to what God is saying to us from the world.

It is in the framework of the second factor that we should see the significance of "coffee shops."[12] It may well be, that as well as dialogue groups in particular sociological structures, there are needed many relatively unstructured listening points which will enable Christians to hear as well as to speak, and which will witness to the world that the Church is willing to take *their* concerns seriously.

In both types of groups, however—unstructured listening points and groups formed around specific concerns of the

12. For example, in the Church of the Savior, Washington, D. C.; and in the Presbyterian Church, Burlington, Vermont.

world—dialogue will be a primary form of the relationship.

EXAMPLES: 1. URBAN STRUCTURES

In his book "The Secular Relevance of the Church," Gayraud S. Wilmore describes how a Presbyterian Minister in Chicago, Robert Christ, with a small group of laymen took the initiative in creating

> "the Organization for the Southwest Community (OSC) in the southwest corner of Chicago covering fifteen square miles and populated by over 200,000 people, 18,000 of whom are Negroes. This organization, whose community 'congress' represents several smaller groups of residents, social agencies, and businessmen, some of whom were originally organized to 'keep the Negroes out,' is a result of the decision of the citizens of southwest Chicago to stabilize their community on an integrated basis and to determine its life. In 1960 it had a budget of $50,000 and a professional staff of five. Its program committees included Real Estate Practices, Home Loan, Urban Renewal, Safety, Education, Traffic and Transportation, and other aspects of life in a heterogeneous, dynamic urban community.
>
> "The role of the Seventh Church, twenty-five other Protestant congregations, and eleven Roman Catholic parishes is set forth in a report Robert Christ made in 1961 to a conference of inner-city pastors. The report reads in part: 'Seventh Church's early involvement enabled it to have a formative influence on OSC programs and policies. To affect the nature of community organization the local church must be represented at the time and place at which basic policy is set, boundaries established, membership determined (attempts were made to exclude Negroes living in the fringe neighborhoods) and staff hired. . . . By the time of the second congress a caucus of Protestant ministers was established . . . the caucus selected a "Protestant

spokesman" and "floor leader" and functioned effectively enough to assure a concerted, positive Protestant voice.'

"The OSC had a stormy beginning, with the residential segregation question dividing the membership and charges of 'communism' and 'fascism,' and other bitterly contested issues threatening to blow the organization and the tense community apart. A Methodist minister and vice-president of the organization was forced from his church; the Seventh Church lost membership and finances as a result of the withdrawal of members who could not accept the role it was playing in 'politics and racial integration.' It is to the credit of the presbytery and the United Presbyterian Board of National Missions that the congregation was supported financially and not abandoned to the disintegrating consequences of losing about 15 per cent of its membership.

"But neither was Robert Christ abandoned by the central core of his laymen. He speaks of the important role of the church session and the impossibility of being able to continue the work without 'the elders' understanding of urban problems and the church's mission. Commenting upon the deepening faith that was experienced by the laity, he writes: 'Because participation in the OSC has made the Church's faith relevant and immediately applicable, involvement in community has resulted in growth in the faith for numerous laymen and ministers. The important implications of the gospel have become apparent; under stress the church's faith begins to flourish, confrontation with the cost of discipleship creates discipleship. Churchmen involved have declared, "Now the Church is getting down to business"; 'Do they (the critics) expect Christians to do anything other than be concerned about our community?'

"The existence of an effective community organization supplies a channel for the Christian's concern for the neighbor. Instead of preaching love of the brother and redemption of life, and then stuttering when laymen ask 'How?' the Church now has an instrument for the expression of obedience. Conscientious laymen need not feel guilty and hypocritical because they have no effective means of practicing what they profess. Provided with a realistic channel for discipleship, Christians will practice, and grow in their faith.

"Robert Christ makes another interesting observation about the new spirit that came to the laymen of Seventh Church despite the fact that it had to pare down its program, [and] eliminate much of the inbuilding 'program' of the conventional Presbyterian church. . . .

"Active participation in community life has supplied an instrument for the local church to have an impact on mass society; the church has a tool for positively influencing the attitudes and conduct of the many people with whom it has had no direct contact. The visible signs of the renewal of the congregational and community life gave the church a sense of accomplishment, an awareness that it could and was doing something of significance. The effort, cost, and consequences of full participation in communal life compel the local church to rethink its mission to the city and the world. The demands and the controversies of organizing the southwest community have resulted in men taking the prominent role in this undertaking of the church; relatively few women were involved in the first two years (1959 and 1960) of the OSC.

"Certainly no conclusions can yet be written concerning the ultimate significance of the decision of this particular church to move into the vortex of the turbulent and always potentially violent situation caused by the sociological transition of southwest Chicago. But it is clear that the Seventh Church has shown a path which can lead to the renewal of community life and of the church itself. As Robert Christ has said, 'Mission does not just happen.' It requires a group of people, an intelligence and reconnaissance vanguard that will also provoke a fair fight when it is strategic. It needs laymen who are called by God for the purpose, trained with all the wisdom and sophistication experience can give, and who are willing to take the risks of using the forms of power available to them to do the works of love."[13]

When the Church commits herself to this kind of servant action in the world, there necessarily arises the question as to how the Church can bring to this dialogue the dimension of reflection upon the goals of action in the light of God's purpose.[14] One aspect of this needed reflection is clear: the necessity for bringing the action within the awareness of Christ's Lordship and for seeing all human action within the renewing context of his forgiving grace. But when we explore the meaning of this Lordship of Christ for action within the secular realms, important questions arise as to the way in which "secular" goals find their true place within the total purpose of Christ to gather to himself a new humanity united in his love, within the framework of a redeemed creation.

We can illustrate something of what is involved here by referring to a debate that is being waged at present concerning the way the Church ought to relate to the academic world in the universities. Quite a number of leaders in the campus Christian ministry (influenced by Bonhoeffers's contention that "the world has come of age" and that "secular" realms of life, now having gained their independent secular status, can at last fulfil their God-given role), are

---

13. Gayraud S. Wilmore, "The Secular Relevance of the Church," The Westminster Press, pp. 80-83. (Quoted by permission)

14. Gibson Winter in "The New Creation as Metropolis," *op. cit.*, p. 72, puts this well:

> "The servant Church is not simply serving men on their terms; it serves God by ministering in judgment and promise within the structures of man's world. The laity is, thus, the prophetic fellowship which summons men to reflection upon their responsibility for shaping the future. This prophetic fellowship has no special program or political party; it has only the commitment to the New Mankind which God has created in his Son, the mankind of love and reconciliation which discloses the true being of all men and their life together."

insisting that the Christian ministry in the university must begin with "dialogue" in the context of the proper concerns of the academic world. They believe that this requires a revolution in the Church's approach.

Arthur Brandenburg[15] quotes a statement from Franklin Littell which gives the judgment of this group on present American Christian student work: "On most campuses it is a leisure-time activity in 'homes away from home,' chiefly attractive to students who are not otherwise integrated into campus life (in fraternities, athletics, dramatics and the like). It has little to do with the students' real concerns; and almost nothing to do with the educational process which is going on." He then insists that the Christian dialogue must take the secular academic commitment and the proper concerns of students with full seriousness. When that happens, says Brandenburg, it is likely "that we shall have on our hands more obsolete buildings than we shall ever know how to use." The present place of Church "foundations" on the edge of the campus in expensive centers is symbolic of its failure to take seriously the secular integrity of the academic world.

What then is the way in which the Church witnesses, in this dialogue, to the Lordship of Christ? Brandenburg suggests that an approach to a true Christian dialogue is offered by the North Carolina Community of Lay Scholars who have sought an answer in a "style of life" which expresses their faith in and obedience to the Lordship of Christ and yet gives them a free corporate structure which enables them to move into the academic sphere. This style of life he calls a "worldly monasticism."

EXAMPLES: 2. THE WORLD OF ART

The Rev. Howard Moody of Judson Memorial Church

15. In a M.S.M. pamphlet called: "A Community of Lay Scholars in North Carolina," written by Arthur Brandenburg.

in Greenwich Village, New York, has tried to lead that church into a relation to Greenwich Village based on the belief that "the world should be allowed to write the agenda." Since the characteristic of the most distinctive groups in the area is concern with the arts, Judson Memorial has sought to accept these groups in their worldly integrity; allowing a dialogue to develop on the basis of the questions and strivings of the group. The first movement in the church's relation to these communities of art is not one of judgment or even question, but one of listening (and looking) and acceptance—in itself an expression of Christ's attitude to the world and an affirmation of the Church's recognition of the God-given mission of the artist. A second movement in the relation can then emerge. Once their apprehension of life is taken seriously and the integrity of their calling is recognized, then the opportunity is given for the meaning of their God-given ministry to be discussed and disclosed within the dialogue.

In a Report of a special committee appointed by the National Council of Churches (U.S.A.) to examine the role of the Council in relation to the arts, there is an affirmation of the need for the Church to have a positive listening relation to the world of the arts, on the ground that the very calling of the artists enables them to speak to the Church concerning her contemporary mission.

> "The church is concerned with the arts because the church is concerned with the concrete actuality of human life. The church has a given charter, a message, and a mission; and she is commanded to fulfil her charter, proclaim her message, and obey her mission in full identification with men's deeds and dreams and struggles and hurts.
>
> "The church's obedience, therefore, must be wrought out ever anew in absolute company with the changing facts of man's situation. If she is to speak helpfully of health, she must know man's sickness and his hurt; if she is to

speak of the peace of God, she must make true soundings of the angers of men.

"The full scope of Christian life and work, therefore, inevitably includes attention to the arts in all their contemporary forms. We may distinguish, and not always properly, between religious and secular art, between the fine arts and the practical arts, between the traditional arts and the mass media of today. Nevertheless, all such esthetic expressions must be included in the territory to which Christian responsibility for the life of men directs itself. The arts, old and new, good and bad, are peculiarly carriers of meaning and value in our society as in all societies. Thus the arts and the meanings symbolized and communicated have obvious religious and theological significance."

Behind this Report there lies a vital theological principle; the same principle that is assumed in the approach of Judson Memorial Church. God speaks, it is assumed, not only from the past in the history of redemption and in the present through the religious life of the church; he also speaks from the world. This speaking from the world—attested to in Scripture in the long line of pagan witnesses—requires the Church to have its *ears* attuned outwards to hear what God is saying from the world, and its *eyes* focussed on the world to see where God is calling us to cooperate with what he is doing in his creation. This word and work of God that are to be heard and seen in the world have to do with God's total purpose for his cosmos—a purpose which is expressed in Scripture as the redemption and fulfillment of the world of men and nature.

The Report expressed the belief that the church has all too often been so concerned with its internal life, so deaf and blind to God's work in the world and so unaware of God's purpose for the natural, that there has been a large scale alienation of the artist from the church.

"It is precisely because Christian faith has so often failed to understand and affirm the godliness of the natural, and affirm grace as having within its scope and intention the holy evaluation and restoration of the natural that the artists (avid children of the immediacy of the natural) have come to regard themselves and feel themselves regarded as pagan celebrators of the godless."

If this is so, then we can see the importance of the dialogue relation being attempted by Judson Memorial Church. But this raises again the question as to how the Church may fulfil its proper role in the dialogue—how its "marks" may be manifest and its witness fulfilled? The N.C.C. Report suggests:

1. That the church must accept responsibility for "the estrangement that presently exists between the world of the artist and the world of the Christian faith." The church must witness to Christ's "acceptance," and this acceptance must be offered by the church to this (and to the other communities of the world) in such a way that the integrity of their community is respected.[16]

---

16. A passage in the Report deserves to be quoted because of the powerful way in which it expresses the importance *to the church* of this listening relationship to the world of the artists:

"The artist loves the world. And because he wants to penetrate to the world's secret he cannot be content with obvious, merely surface appearances. To dig at 'what lies under what lies under the shell' is the anguished confession of his resolute love. This loving faithfulness to the world may cause the artist to be harsh; it certainly means that he must select. All selection is a reduction in order to specify the particular and the significant; and such a process necessitates what the quick look will call distortion. But this distortion is not perverse or without sober intent; it is a turning and a twisting and a peeling-back to the end that the artist may find and state some truer, deeper, fuller, form by which to declare his love.

"From this immediacy of love the artist cannot tear himself loose. He is bound to the world. Whether he deals with the world in forms that are harmonious or dissonant, forms that disclose an ideal or a bitter vision, the bondage remains. And all his efforts are ultimately a kind of tender celebration.

"Thus deeply covenanted to the world the artist often regards the Christians he meets with bewilderment, or incomprehension, or

2. That there is, however, a necessary two-sidedness in the Church's relation to the world. The dialogue should be such that the role of the artist is brought within the message of judgment and redemption; and in such a way that the vocation of the artist can be disclosed.

> "The call to 'test the spirits,' to 'discern the thoughts and intents of the heart,' to 'cast down imagination and every high thing that is exalted against the knowledge of God' and to bring 'every thought into captivity to the obedience of Christ'—this call is imperative in an age like ours. . . .
>
> "Christian discrimination at work upon contemporary literature and the arts will not be chiefly negative. A vanguard of Christian intellectuals, artists and critics will render one of its greatest services in identifying and proclaiming the extraordinary wealth of wisdom and insight in contemporary 'secular' work. Modern movements in the arts represent often a healthful protest against meagerness or vitiation in the spiritual life of Christendom, a witness to elements of the Christian tradition neglected by the church, as well as clues to a needed contemporary reformulation of the faith. The church must be hospitable to such insights and furnish itself with groups qualified to mediate them to all Christians."

---

anger, or disgust. For they seem to know another world, an exclusively non-natural grace, a life which seems somehow to inform them and sustain them whose immediacy is not his, and which looks upon his passion and work with uninterest or disdain. Their love has no commerce with his; their 'good' seems to go its own way with no valuation, or even a negative valuation, of his 'good.' They seem to him not really to care for the immediacies of the world as such—but only to care for what they can do with such immediacies, how they can use them, or manage them, dispose them for ends unrelated to the sheer vitality and the primal urgency of things themselves.

"In this 'distance' between the artist in the world and the Christian believer in the world some profound and fatal misunderstanding is at work. The roots of this strange malformation of the minds of the two communities are many and deep; and while it is not the task of this report to disclose, interpret, and correct them, nothing less than such an effort must be the core of whatever continuing reflection and action is proposed and implemented."

The question as to the form the dialogue must take so that the two aspects of "acceptance" and "judgment" may be truly expressed (and so that the "structure" may not be "heretical") is one of real urgency. The relation of Word and Sacrament to the dialogue process; the suggestion that Christians through forms of fellowship directly related to the community concerned should reveal a "style of life" that is a sign of Christ's Lordship; these are questions needing deep consideration.

In the East German Working Group they asked what are some of the criteria of "true" as opposed to "heretical" structures. They gave it as their experience that the congregation is truly Christian when it is seen as a gathering which takes place "for the purpose of sending"; a community of mutual responsibility in which the resources of the Word and Sacraments enable the members of the fellowship to help each other with their important daily decisions. For this reason they concluded that "concern for congregational renewal must not be directed exclusively toward the traditional picture of the local congregation under the care of a pastor. We must be ready to build a congregation which may have some other form."

Our only question here is as to whether it is still not a remnant of the old concept of localized congregation to maintain such a strict contrast between gathering and sending. Is it not possible that sometimes these two can coalesce? But in any case the East German line of thought would seem to suggest that we must adjust our thinking to include under the concept "congregation" any gathering of Christians which is called by Christ to witness to his Lordship in particular areas of the world's life; and that just as this can occur in residence, so it also can occur in other "worlds" such as art. A "structure" is "heretical" then, if it short circuits the witness to Christ's Lordship over the real "worlds" in which men live.

Following this line of thought we can understand a further insistence in the East German report, that Word and Sacrament are not "truly preached" and "duly administered" unless they are expressions of Christ's living relationship to this real world where the church is called to witness.

> "Pure preaching does not occur when we limit ourselves to the recitation of biblical formulae and the presentation of dogmatically correct teachings. Proper administration of the sacraments does not simply consist in the performance of liturgically correct actions.
>
> "True proclamation of the Gospel exists only where the proclaimer ceases to consider himself exclusively as the giver and begins to seek Christ in communion and living encounter with his fellow men. In this confrontation he will constantly summon and guide his fellow-members of the congregation to a responsible and critical hearings of the proclamation.
>
> "The minister is also a member of the congregation. He too, like all the others, is in need of the Word, the sacraments, the charismata and the spiritual experiences which have been given to the congregation. Further, true proclamation of the Gospel comes only with his readiness to take seriously the questions and assaults of the world and the congregation and not to withdraw into the safety of the pulpit, the lecture-stand or the manse.
>
> "True administration of the sacraments exists only where they are no longer considered as gifts offered to isolated individuals, but where pastor and congregation, through the sacraments, take seriously their appointment to create, strengthen and maintain fellowship with the Lord and among themselves in their everyday life. A biblically-oriented use of the sacraments is called into question not only by false teaching but perhaps even more by the loveless lives of Christians who participate in the Lord's Supper (cf. I Cor. 11:17ff). A biblically-oriented administration of the sacraments demands not only a pure proclamation of the meaning of the sacraments and proper forms of

their celebration but also a vital fellowship among those who share in them."

The East German report then summarizes what they believe to be the characteristics of a "true" congregation of the Word and Sacrament in their setting. Their answer reflects a modern form of the relation between the "instituted" and "prudential" means of grace which we discussed in Chapter 3.

"Such a congregation, having become a community of fellowship through the Word and Sacrament, will express itself by:

a) gathering as familia Dei in a commonly formed worship service;
b) common reading and study of the Bible in small and large groups;
c) daily devotion by which—even if it takes place at home—we constantly renew our place in the congregation;
d) intercession based on an exchange of specific concerns;
e) mutual visitation and becoming acquainted with one another;
f) practical assistance in financial and personal affairs (sickness, education, money, etc.);
g) mutual advice in important and difficult decisions of daily life (political, occupational and family questions);
h) reciprocal consolation, strengthening and admonition;
i) common responsibility for the life and structure of the congregation.

"On the whole, we might say that the congregation as a community of fellowship assumes the form of a brotherhood."

At this point we should add that the form of the Church's dialogue relation with the world has different dimensions in East Germany than in West Germany or in the U.S.A. Their chance for a more structured dialogue with various aspects of their society—such as art, politics, business—is more limited; and for that reason, the congregational forms may well be different. But in each case we face the same theological questions as to what constitutes a true witnessing form of the church's relation to the world. And the suggestion they give is that there are necessary "marks" of the Christian relationship—Word and Sacraments are "given" forms of witness to Christ's Lordship—but that these "given" forms themselves are meant to give their witness to Christ's living Lordship in the context of a dialogue relation to the world's questions.

An illustration of the "dialectical" relationship between the Church taking form around a need that arises in the world, and yet bringing to that need the transcendent reality of the grace of our Lord Jesus Christ, is provided by the experience of the Reverend Lynn Hageman in ministering to adolescent drug addicts in New York. He could witness strongly to the necessity for the Church to see herself as "event," finding ever new expression at the point where Christ calls forth a witness to his living Lordship in responsive service to changing forms of need. But he also discovered the reality of the church as "institution." He found that in the "givenness" of the liturgy, and in the symbolic contact of the world of grace with the reality of nature, in the Sacraments, communication took place that went beyond the possibilities of human "dialogue."[17] Here

---

17. Reginald Fuller in his article "Liturgy and Devotion" in "The Place of Bonhoeffer," Association Press, p. 179, quotes Bonhoeffer's statement that communication of the gospel must not be by words simply, but by being. "The church is her true self only when she exists for humanity. . . . She must take her part in the social life of the world, not lording it over men, but helping and serving the world." This is what Bonhoeffer called "being there for others." Fuller then comments:

> "Now there is a real danger that some may take the bit between their teeth and as they read Bonhoeffer come to the conclusion—the old liberal conclusion—that the business of the church is to become a social welfare organization. But 'being there for others,' as Bonhoeffer means it, is a witness to God's being there for us in Jesus Christ: and this will only be seen where the church's being there for others constantly springs from her own interior life in which God is

was given a sacred sign in the midst of the secular which witnessed to the fact that Christ's redeeming presence transcends the flux of time—not as standing outside of time, but as standing within time; anchored within the daily world of bread and wine in such a way that it speaks of Christ's willingness to save the world from its tendency to fall into chaos by giving the lost a saving participation in the fullness of his love.

EXAMPLES: 3. THE STRUGGLE FOR PEACE

We spoke of the crisis needs which should call forth structured response from the Church—such as race, housing, poverty and war. It seems clear here that the Church at present has failed to find the way to form itself to participate as it should in the world's struggle for peace.[18]

---

constantly 'there' for her as he was there in Christ, in the Word and sacraments. In other words, it needs liturgy—that point where the church is being truly herself, the community for whom God in Christ is there for her at the center—for the kind of evangelism and social service that Bonhoeffer proposes. Otherwise it will become merely human and humanitarian. Undoubtedly it is this kind of evangelism going hand in hand with a social concern, the witness of the Christian church being the church in the community in which it is set, that must be the evangelism of the future. And here liturgy, as the focal point of the church's life, must be at the heart of it."

One can only add that there seems to be a good case for insisting that the liturgy too needs to reflect our "being there for others" through identification with the rhythms of modern life in language, music and action. It is true Christian liturgy when the "given" shape of the gospel of God's redeeming action takes us up into itself by coming to us in the midst of the shape of our life.

18. Just so also it has failed to form itself in such a way as to participate in the struggle for racial equality. The isolation of the races from each other in the structures of the church can well be judged "heretical." It has meant that the church has reflected the world's demonic patterns of race separation and has failed to develop forms of church life that witness to Christ's reconciling love. It has meant too that when the struggle for racial justice has reached crisis points (as in South Africa and in the U.S.A.) the church found that it was not free to participate in that struggle by giving a direct witness to unity in

Christ, even when it desired to do so. This has been the tragedy in the U.S.A. in 1963. The forms the church has needed for its witness were lacking. Instead the church found itself to be a prisoner of its own (and the world's) "heretical" structures.

As this was being prepared for printing, however, the General Board of the N.C.C. (U.S.A.) took an action which could possibly represent a major breakthrough in *the way the Church responds to God's missionary call from the world.* Here is the Resolution:

> "The General Board requests the President of the N.C.C., immediately to appoint a Commission on Religion and Race. This Commission shall have the following purposes:
>
> To focus the concern, the conviction, the resources and the action of the member communions in issues of religion and race;
>
> To provide a national interdenominational liaison with interfaith and other concerted efforts;
>
> To focus and mobilize the resources of the units of the N.C.C.;
>
> To assist the nation to see this crisis in its moral dimension. . . .
>
> The General Board authorizes this commission to make commitments, call for actions, take risks on behalf of the N.C.C. which are required by the situation and are consistent both with the substance and the implications of the actions and decisions of the N.C.C. in the area of religion and race. The authorization of the Commission includes:
>
> 1. The encouragement of negotiations, demonstrations, and direct action in places of particular crisis.
> 2. The mobilization of resources to encourage legislative and executive acts in order to bring dignity, equality and justice to all Americans.
> 3. The mobilization of the resources of the churches in order to put their own house in order by desegregating all the institutions of the church.
> 4. The development and implementation of long term plans and strategies so that a continuing design of action will move us steadily towards the moral goal of full human rights for all."

What is the significance of this? That a responsible Church body has officially broken *free* from its own *internal* machinery, in response to God's urgent call from *the needs of the world,* and has offered to allow itself to find its servant form around this worldly need. That is a miracle of grace! Of course, there is danger that an action of freedom taken in reply to the urgent cry of God from the world may be one from which the church leaders will be tempted to shrink. They may wish to return to the fleshpots of their Egyptian captivity as slaves to safe procedural action. And, of course too, there is danger that risks of action out in the world may lead to error and failure. But at least the risks are in this case risks of relevance; not the risks of the present irrelevance. (Continued)

When we ask, however, what are the structures the Church needs in order to be able to witness to God's mission to bring peace on earth, we find ourselves singularly unprepared.

We can suggest certain requirements:

i) The structures must be such that the Church takes seriously the decision making centers.
ii) They must be such that this Christian concern finds a way of relating itself to the non-Christian concern for peace; but in this identification finding also ways of witnessing to the content that as Christians we believe belongs to the word "peace."
iii) They must be such that the struggle for peace can find expression in particular calls for action. This is difficult for Christians, because there are at present unresolved conflicts concerning the type of witness that is demanded of us. But this difficulty should make it all the more imperative for us to discover structures which would give us channels of action by enabling us

a) To assess the level of present agreement in the Church. A comparison of the encyclical of Pope John XXIII

When the church is drawn out to allow itself to form around the signs of God's action in the world of need, then the problem of *theological judgment* becomes acute: What is true "church action"? But now theological problems arise in their right context—the context of involvement in the mission of Christ as his servant people.

A further significant possibility here opened up, is that there becomes possible *a meeting* of *the forms of new missionary life* that are appearing at this crisis point in the world—forms with their rediscovery of life under the cross; with their reaching out to new liturgical forms, new hymns, new means of mutual care, in bodies such as the Southern Christian Leadership Conference—*with the official national and denominational* life of the churches. We have spoken at several points of the need for the "ecclesiolae" at particular points of witness and service, to be brought into relation with forms of church life that draw them together and allow the wider unity of life in Christ to be proclaimed. Here opportunity has been given for this type of relation to develop. The big question now is: will the churches be free enough to support the necessary action when it lies outside their ordered forms?

("Peace on Earth") with the statements of the World Council of Churches does reveal a marked degree of general agreement which should become the basis for developing forms of church life which would provide for joint action for peace on this basis; and for co-operative action with non-Christians.

b) To press on urgently toward the resolution of continuing disagreement. Is it not reasonable to suggest that the absence of any structures to provide for this urgent task is "heretical"?

c) To plan and to take specific action as responsible church action, in co-operation with any non-Christians who desire to work with us. Such structures would need to take seriously the realities of the power structures of the world, and the need to influence the centers of decision-making.

When we contemplate the need for such a form of church life, we are quickly forced back upon the theological question of the nature of "the world" in which the servant task of the Church must be performed. We are forced to ask about the forms that evil assumes—the nature of "principalities and powers." We are forced to ask about the nature of Christ's victory over the forces of evil, and how the Church is expected to witness to this victory of Christ, and to be a sign of that victory.

The conclusions which are reached here will affect decisions as to the forms the church needs to assume in order to fulfill her mission. And fortunately, there is no need to start *de novo* in a discussion of these questions. We can use the ecumenical studies already undertaken in this area. The W.C.C. document "The Lordship of Christ Over the Church and the World" includes a section (pp. 21-27): "What is meant by Christ's victory over the 'powers'? How can we give meaning to this in the modern world?" The answers suggested are not claimed as complete; and the "structures" of the church related to action in crisis areas such as peace, race, poverty, housing, will need to provide for continuing reflection on such theological issues which will affect the nature of our Christian witness. Nevertheless the preliminary conclusions still suggest a great deal for the forms of our obedience. Take, e.g., this statement:

> "The 'powers' are seen, especially in the Pauline letters, as representing the universe, and their reality cannot simply be identified with the power of sin, but must be taken to include everything exercising power over man: physical, historical, social, psychical, para-psychical and ideological factors. On the other hand, the enslaving power of these realities cannot be isolated from human sin. The 'powers and principalities' are known to us only as powers of a world in opposition to Christ, and we cannot with any significant meaning talk about a corruption of the order and nature of the world, without at the same time talking about the sin of man, by which his relation to the created and ordered world has been corrupted. Some divergence of opinion exists as to the question of whether the reality of the powers and their hostility against God can be interpreted in merely 'existential' terms or not. Is the New Testament idea of the opposition of the 'powers' to be interpreted as a mythical way of stating the frightful mystery of man's sinful opposition to God? Or is the order of nature in which man lives, not only as a personal being, but as a species of mammal, also of importance in this connection? In any case, the hostility of the 'powers' indicates the total, trans-subjective dimensions of sin as a power dominating man even against his own knowledge and will, and operating not only in the individual, but also in society and in the whole history of mankind."

Here we see that *at least* we are required *to locate those "trans-subjective" forms of sin that dominate man in society; in order that we may then seek to reveal Christ's victory over the powers*. This point the document affirms:

"According to the biblical view the enthroned and victorious Christ is reigning when he struggles against his enemies and overcomes them (I Cor. 15:25, cf. Ch. V). It may also be stressed that Christ, as the Lord and Head of all powers is Lord over space and time (Rom. 8: 38, 39), whereas we are still living in this world of space and time in which the 'powers' are exercising their dominion, and attacking man as powers of temptation.

"A possible line of approach seems to be the following one: Man, created in the image of God, is created to rule on earth. Trying to assert himself in opposition to the will of God, and worshipping the creature instead of the Creator, man no longer rules, but is ruled and becomes enslaved under the powers which he worships. In Christ, conquering in temptation, on the cross and in the resurrection, man is again ruling, Christ being himself the 'image of God' (Mark 1:12-13; Col. 1:15-20). Christ's victory over the powers is shared by man, in so far as he by faith becomes a 'new man' in Christ, and is made free from the domination of the powers. This includes the knowledge that:

"a) We are delivered from the kingdom of darkness and transferred to the kingdom of God's beloved Son (Col. 1:13); our sins are forgiven, we are made free from the curse and the letter of the Law, and made members of Christ, in the Church which is his body (Gal. 3:6-4:11; Eph. 2; Col. 1:12-23; 2:6-15).

"b) No power whatsoever can separate us from the love of God in Christ (Rom. 8:38-39).

"c) No power, asserted by any 'philosophy' or human 'tradition,' can add anything to what has already been given in Christ and, therefore, claim any worship or ultimate loyalty (Col. 1:9-2:4). Accordingly, any kind of legalism is incompatible with the Gospel (Gal. 4:8-10).

"d) The believer is not taken out of the world, but through his participation in the death of Christ, he has died to the 'elemental spirits of the world' and is thus free from slavery under them, and is free to make use of all good things which God has created (Col. 2:20-23; cf. Chapter II).

"e) The victory of Christ means hope and help in our struggle against temptations caused by the world and its powers (Eph. 6:10-17; Heb. 2:14-18).

"f) Where, through the name and power of Christ, health, order and welfare in the life of individuals and society are restored, this can be seen as a sign of the victory which Christ has won and shall win. But within the sphere of empiric facts, no definite victory is ever won; the possibility mentioned in Matt. 12:43-45 always has to be kept in mind."

This would suggest that the church now, in this "time between the times," participates in Christ's victory over the evil powers in an incomplete way. We wait for our final deliverance, but in the meantime witness to that deliverance *by witnessing in the form of our life and service to our faith in Christ's victory.*

Take an example in the area of race. Here we see a modern demonic structure in the way race prejudice and hostility takes on organized social forms so that people find themselves imprisoned by it and swept along by it even when they would like to be free of it. As we see, for example, the panic of people when they are confronted with the possibility of their protected residential community being invaded by Negroes, and as we see reasonably good people erupt into violence in reaction to that "threat" to their prejudice, we know we are facing a demonic structure of evil. It is important, however, to see that far from enabling the church to witness to Christ's victory over that demonic structure, the present form of church life (largely isolated in the segregated pattern of residence communities) more often expresses the imprisonment of the church's life within those demonic structures. Wilmore gives a particular example:

> "A group of Presbyterian elders who were also realtors in a Pittsburgh community were asked by their pastor to open the way for a cultured Negro family to purchase a home in their neighborhood. After a lengthy discussion in which they consulted Scripture, prayed and generally agonized over a decision, they summoned their minister and reported: 'Our duty is clear. We know that as Christian men we ought to give the word that would make it possible for this man to find a house here, but, God help us, we cannot do it. Most of us have spent a life time building up our businesses. The reprisals from the realty board, the banks, and certain other groups would be more than we could take and stay in business. Not only our businesses but our families would suffer all kinds of threats and social ostracism. We just can't do what we know we ought to do as Christians.' "[19]

The clear conclusion would seem to be that the Church must develop forms which will help Christians to meet this conflict between the obedience they see and the world's pressure against that obedience. A witnessing form of church life is needed which takes the demonic structure seriously and girds itself for action against it in witness to the Lordship of Christ. Wilmore comments:

> "In so far as people in our culture act in segmentalized roles as defined and required by organized groups able to apply social and economic power, the church that makes no demands upon its members, gives them no stronghold from which to fight, and is afraid to use its own institutional power when it is necessary is simply eliminated from the struggle."[20]

At this point, we must raise two further major questions.

---

19. G. Wilmore, *op. cit.,* pp. 49-50.
20. *Ibid.,* p. 51.

A NEW MONASTICISM?

When we seek to assess the "principalities and powers" against which we wrestle in the name Christ, we have to ask ourselves: What is meant in Ephesians when it speaks of our witness *to* the principalities and powers? Are we to think of the mysterious powers of evil as more than the forms they assume in the world?[21] What is the nature of our spiritual battle against them? About the fourth century, as soon as the church took on responsibility for direct witness to Christ in the social structures of the world, there also developed the monasteries where the monks looked upon themselves as front line troops in the battle against the demonic forces. If the church were to battle them effectively in the social forms they took in the city of man, then the monks must go out to the desert and meet the demons in the spiritual wilderness where they gather their forces for the attack on the city. By their constant prayer they carried on that battle on the frontier as indispensable partners of those who were engaged in the battle in society.

In Taize, Reformed monks are now seeking to combine these two roles in the one monastic order. Some of their number are sent on missions of servant identification into the cities such as Lyons, while the rest remain within the monastic life of prayer for the church and the world. Similarly there is in the Church of England a renewal of monasticism, often with a determined attempt to maintain a similar servant identification with the needs of the world.

If this assessment of the reality of evil is justified, then it may be that the church is heretical in form if it does not possess such centers witnessing to the fact that in this world our battle against principalities and powers is always incomplete, and that we must engage in this battle

---

21. Paul Minear "Horizons of Christian Community," Association Press, p. 55.

as those who constantly pray for the final manifestation of the victory of Christ and who witness to this hope by forms of life that surround our continuing battle in the world with these symbols of the hope that lies beyond our battle, in the victory of Christ.

A HIERARCHICAL PATTERN OF CHURCH LIFE?

The need for forms of church life reaching out in dialogue relationship to men in the various sociological structures, in communities of concern and need, and in social crisis situations requiring group response, points to the call for the development of what the East Germans call "brotherhood groups" and Americans often call "koinonia groups." So far we have asked what characteristics such groups must reveal in order to express the "given" nature of the gospel and the "presence" of Christ at particular points of need. In such group identification, cells of church life would develop in the broken and separated parts of our culture. But this then raises difficulties.

Is it not likely that these church cells will sometimes find it difficult to communicate with each other? How can the unity of the body of Christ transcending these separations be made manifest? Can "hierarchical" forms be developed which express this wider unity and which also allow for the planning that is necessary to direct our Christian obedience across cultural, national, racial and other lines? The ecumenical development in refugee and relief work made necessary, for example, the development of a church structure to express this ministry.[22] If the peace problem is to find forms necessary to direct Christian action

22. The "Joint Action For Mission" project of the Division of World Mission and Evangelism of the W.C.C. is an attempt to discover further ecumenical forms of church life which will enable us better to share our resources in such a way that our servant life can be related more effectively to the changing patterns of the world's need. The developments in this area are of great potential importance.

to the points of decision in society, then there would be needed some similar hierarchical structure. We must raise, too, the question of whether the growing inter-dependence of modern urban society—together with its more marked "sub-cultures"—does not require a co-ordinate form of church life which combines the two approaches: the "cell" approach to sub-cultures and the co-ordinated planned approach in some modern diocesan form which will develop the common forms of life needed in a segment of a city in order to reveal the unity of life in Christ, and the unity also in Christ's plan for his world; a unity that transcends the isolations of the "sub-cultures."[23]

---

23. In Chapter 1 we referred to a "sector plan" in which a serious attempt would be made to combine the approach to sub-cultures with the development of forms of life that transcend these divisions and manifest the unity of life in Christ. We referred also to Bishop J. A. T. Robinson's suggestion for a "joint episcopacy." The need for such expressions of trans-cultural unity would seem to call for responsible experimentation on this level as well.

A present development like the Urban Training Center in Chicago which is making a thoroughly planned long term attack upon the alienation of the church from so much of urban life and is training clergy and laity for a new engagement in this "lost world" is of the utmost importance. But it would seem obvious that so far very little is yet being done to train lay ministries for either the particular sociological areas of modern life, or to train clergy to work with the laity in these areas and to bring them together as well in the larger unity of the church. We are only at the beginning of the developments that are necessary.

The patent need for such planning to be ecumenical must be faced. This will require a new step forward in the understanding of the conciliar movement. To such familiar functions as being "forums" for furthering inter-church contact, or agencies for joint action in social service, or co-operative bodies for joint studies, we must recognize further necessary roles of bodies like a W.C.C., and an N.C.C.; including the forging of united forms of lay witness in the unities of the world's sociological segments. All such roles are "temporary" until unity is given by Christ to his Church; but we should remember that it is only as we act together according to the common visions that Christ has granted us, that we will receive that fuller vision that he may be waiting to grant, in order to lead us into that organic unity which would make conciliar bodies of the inter-confessional kind unnecessary.

Here we can do no more than raise these questions. The questions are important—they arise from the gospel itself as it forces us to reflect on the relation of the church to our mobile world. Perhaps the dreams for that type of hierarchical life in the church which would rise in architectonic fashion from the cells of identification with men in their particular needs and concerns, to the ever increasing levels of form which would enable the church to express the dynamic purpose of Christ to gather all men and all things into the unity of his divine life: forms, therefore, which rise above class difference, racial difference, national difference: perhaps such dreams are beyond realization in time. But dream them we must. And as we dream, we must pray that God will give us that measure of present realization of these dreams which will enable the Church to be a true sign of God's mission; in order that the world may believe. And as we pray, we must seek to be obedient.

QUESTIONS

1. If Christ is Lord over the world and the Church, how can we assist the Church to recognize this fact, and to accept its implications and live by them?
2. How accurate is the observation that the Church is a "slice of the world" that is different only in that it knows its Creator and Redeemer?
3. How has that knowledge and acceptance made a difference in our lives and relationships (II Corinthians 5:17-20)?
4. Where would be "appropriate" gathering places in the world for the Church to manifest God's mission?

5. In what way does God speak through "pagan witnesses"? Is their witness of the same kind as the witness of Christ's disciples? What is the relationship?
6. Is there anything wrong with the Church having a building or gathering place near the residence of a large percentage of its members, and near the schools and playgrounds of many of its children and youth, if it would *also* gather working men near their work and working women at their places of vocation and people near their places of recreation and leisure time, etc.? If both, what should be the relation between the different groups?
7. How can artists, poets, playwrights, actors, musicians, persons involved in the professional entertainment world, newscasters, radio and TV and newspaper people in mass communication, etc., be involved in the mission of the Church?
8. Do such special competencies and vocational opportunities specially equip such persons to interpret the world more accurately to the Church and to bring their variety of gifts as a ministry that the mission of God may permeate all human endeavor?

BIBLIOGRAPHY

1. World Council of Churches documents. (Obtainable in the U.S.A. through Miss Frances Maeda, W.C.C., 4th Floor, 475 Riverside Drive, New York 27, N. Y.)

Concept—a periodical of the Department on Studies in Evangelism. (35 cents per copy)

Bulletins of the Department of the Laity. No. 2-6 are now printed in one volume ($1.00) No. 13 "The Laity: the Church in the World," is also an important study source. (50 cents)

Signs of Renewal. (50 cents)

A Theological Reflection on the Work of Evangelism. (30 cents)

The Missionary Task of the Church: Theological Reflections. (30 cents)

The Lordship of Christ Over the Church and the World. (25 cents)

Christ, the Hope of the World. Report of the Advisory Group. Out of print; but many copies are in circulation.

2. Some Books on the Changing Forms of the Church's Witness.

Hans Margull: "Hope in Action," Fortress, 1961, $5.00. A valuable source for its summary of the thinking on evangelism and related subjects in the major ecumenical documents of the W.C.C. and I.M.C.

Gibson Winter: "The Suburban Captivity of the Churches," Doubleday, 1961, $3.50. "The New Creation as Metropolis," MacMillan, 1963, $3.95. These are stimulating pioneer works exploring the possible new forms of the church's witness in modern urbanized culture.

Peter L. Berger: "The Noise of Solemn Assemblies," Doubleday, 1961, $1.75. Caused quite a stir. Radical criticism of the churches' present irrelevance.

Martin E. Marty: "The New Shape of American Religion," Harper, 1959, $3.50. Less radical than Berger; very readable.

R. C. Johnson (Ed): "The Church and its Changing Ministry," United Presbyterian Church, 510 Witherspoon Bldg., Phila. 7, Pa. $1.00. A study book for 1962 in the United Presbyterian Church, it has a valuable collection of articles related to this study.

Johannes Blauw: "The Missionary Nature of the Church," McGraw Hill, 1962, $3.95. A careful biblical study prepared in relation to the W.C.C. study on "The Missionary Task of the Church."

D. T. Niles: "Upon the Earth," McGraw Hill, 1962, $4.95. Also prepared in relation to the W.C.C. study, it is a valuable analysis of the present evangelistic situation of the Church.

Edwin D. Roels: "God's Mission," Franeker, The Netherlands, T. Wever, 1962.

Harry R. Boer: "Pentecost and Missions," Eerdmans, 1961, $5.00.

3. Special Studies of Experiments or Particular Problems.

G. W. Webber: "God's Colony in Man's World," Abingdon, 1958, $2.75. Written by the leader of the East Harlem Protestant Parish it is already something of a classic in its call to see the church in terms of its mission to the world.

Elizabeth O'Connor: "The Call to Commitment," Harper and Row, 1963, $3.50. Written by the secretary to Gordon Cosby, minister of the Church of the Savior, in Washington, D. C., it is a moving account of another classical attempt to discover relevant missionary forms.

Robert A. Raines: "New Life in the Church," Harper and Row, 1961, $3.00. The story of the renewal of a local church through koinonia groups. Good source for the role of such groups in that framework.

J. Archie Hargreaves: "Stop pussyfooting through a revolution. Some churches that did." United Church of Christ, 1505 Race St., Phila. 2, Pa. (20 cents) Case studies of churches that turned their life outward to take form around particular needs.

Gayraud S. Wilmore: "The Secular Relevance of the Church," Westminster, 1962, $1.25. Its theme is the need for the church to discover its mission in the secular structures of the modern world. Small, but useful.

The Methodist Student Movement has a series of good study papers on the Mission of the Church. Six Study Papers plus Bible Study, available from Dr. G. Martin, P.O. Box 871, Nashville 2, Tenn. (75 cents for set of 6)

[A study in Dutch is sufficiently important to be listed here, even though only a few will be able to read it. *D. Van Swigchem:* "The Missionary Character of the Christian Congregation," Kampen, The Netherlands: J. K. Kok, 1955.]

When reading some of the accounts of experimental places it is easy to receive an idealized picture. This soon vanishes when you come to know them first hand. The "saints" in all of them are also "sinners." Their importance is not that they offer us ideal communities where we might be happier! Their importance must be judged by the extent to which they point the way to the discovery by the church of more relevant ways in which together we may be the servant people of God, participating in the mission of God to his world.